# *Instant*
# COACHING

PAUL BIRCH

**KOGAN
PAGE**

**The Instant Series**

Titles available are:

*Instant Brainpower*, Brian Clegg
*Instant Creativity*, Brian Clegg and Paul Birch
*Instant Interviewing*, Brian Clegg
*Instant Leadership*, Paul Birch
*Instant Motivation*, Brian Clegg
*Instant Negotiation*, Brian Clegg
*Instant Stress Management*, Brian Clegg
*Instant Teamwork*, Brian Clegg and Paul Birch
*Instant Time Management*, Brian Clegg

Available from all good booksellers. For further information on the series please contact the publishers at the address below.

First published in 2001

Kogan Page Limited
120 Pentonville Road
London N1 9JN
UK

Stylus Publishing Inc.
22883 Quicksilver Drive
Sterling VA 20166-2012
USA

**British Library Cataloguing in Publication Data**

A CIP record for this book is available from the British Library.

ISBN 0 7494 3441 4

Typeset by Jo Brereton, Primary Focus, Haslington, Cheshire
Printed and bound in Great Britain by Clays Ltd, St Ives plc

# Contents

# 1

# *WHAT IS COACHING?*

*Let's start at the very beginning. Where better? How would you know coaching if it leapt up and bit you on the ankles? You have no doubt seen coaches at work. You will have been coached. You may even have coached others. Somehow, though, it's the sort of subject that everyone knows about and yet very few people really know.*

There's something about coaching that makes it close to everyone's heart. Talk to anyone about it and they'll have an opinion or a story to tell. Talk to anyone about it and their opinion or story will be different. Indeed, their definitions of coaching will be radically different from one to another. No two people mean the same thing when they talk about coaching. No two people have the same experience of it. No two people will read this book and take away the same messages.

So I'd better make clear my definition of coaching. First, some context. For many the word *coach* is associated with sports and the development of top tennis players, footballers, athletes, etc. This is not my area of expertize, but many of the lessons in this book will be transferable.

For many, thinking of a coach will bring to mind someone who has helped them through some of life's obstacles. This is closer to the area I'll be talking about and many more lessons are transferable from this.

For me, when I am talking about coaching, I am focusing on the world of business. I will be talking about one person in a business helping another to improve their performance.

The way that they do this will vary from situation to situation. It will certainly involve guidance. It will certainly involve an examination of their current performance and the factors that contribute to that performance. It will certainly involve planning changes in performance in a step-by-step manner. It will certainly involve some one-to-one work, even if the coach is working with a group of people. Importantly, the role may or may not be identified as a coach.

You see, I strongly believe that whatever role we play we have the opportunity to coach others. I also believe that we get a great deal more out of life when we take this opportunity and work to improve the skill and ability of those around us. So, whether you have the role of a coach at the moment or not, this book will be useful to you. It will help you to get more out of your life by helping others to get more out of theirs. That sounds altruistic and somehow holier than thou. It is not. You will be able to perform better if those around you perform better. You will be able to excel if you help others to excel. Becoming a coach is also likely to mean that you will become someone that others will start to turn to for guidance and advice.

A coach is not a teacher. A coach does not need to know more or be more highly skilled than the person they coach. Think of a sports coach. They are rarely as good as their star performers and yet they are valued and respected by those stars. They help to improve performance by drawing out the factors that contribute to that performance, whether they know those in advance or not. This makes their role one of questioning. The most powerful tool that a coach has is the question. The right question asked at the right time can do more to move someone forward than any amount of teaching.

This brings us to another fundamental of coaching. Much of what is required is a systematic approach to uncovering what the person being coached knows already.

So, to summarize what coaching is. For me, it is a systematic approach to improvement through questioning and guidance that focuses on incremental changes in current performance to reach a target level. Obviously, as with any definition, it is much more than that and at times much less than that. As you progress through the book, your own definition will develop in relation to your own need to develop coaching skills. Feel free to add to or subtract from my view of coaching because for your circumstances your own definition will be more relevant.

On reflection, the definition I have given of coaching feels far too dry. You see, for me coaching is about helping someone to make their dreams come true. No dry definition is going to sum up the emotions and the passions that this process can arouse. Dreams are at the heart of this book. I may forget that while I'm writing, but I ask you not to. Remember, everything you read about coaching is written in the context of helping someone's dreams to come true.

# 2

# *WHO CAN COACH?*

*Many people see coaching as something that is done by others or is applicable in fields other than their own. This chapter explores the breadth of potential areas for coaching, and looks at those individuals who are well suited and those individuals who are poorly suited to the role of coach.*

We've established that coaches are people like you or me. Some are highly skilled, others can make a difference just by asking the right question of the right person at the right time. There are individuals who are better suited to a coaching role than others. Naturally, this implies that there are individuals who are unsuited to coaching. My belief is that anyone can improve their ability to coach. Some will make this improvement and still not enjoy or shine in the role. When all is said and done, only you can know whether or not this is something that works for you.

There are characteristics that are more likely to incline you to being a better or a worse coach.

Coaches like people. This is a massive generalization because I am sure that there must be excellent coaches who cannot stand being with others. The role of the coach is bound up with others. The coach earns merit through others, not through their own achievements. Someone who doesn't enjoy being with people would find these aspects of the role really tough.

Coaches learn. The coach's role is about questioning and observing and then looking for changes in behaviour that will lead to changes in performance. They must be people who enjoy learning in order to shine at this.

Coaches question, they rarely direct. The popular image of a coach may be the bully in the dressing room shouting abuse at the football team, but such coaches are rare and, in my opinion, poor at their job. The most effective role for a coach to play is that of questioner and observer. When being coached, we are all more likely to take advice that we have generated ourselves than advice that has come from someone else. If your personal style is directive, then you are likely to be suited to the role of team captain rather than coach. (I use team captain here as an analogy. In business there are captains just as there are on the sports field.)

Coaches communicate. One skill that is as important as the questioning is the skill necessary to get a point across. Communication (both ways) is at the heart of the coach's role. This would challenge someone who is a poor communicator.

Coaches give freely. Modern businesses are full of people who guard jealously their small powers. This may be in the form of authority or may be in the form of data and information. Such a person would find coaching difficult because it is inherent in the role that a coach will share what knowledge and ability they have so as to improve whoever they are coaching. They also give of themselves. They give their time, their effort and their ability to help others to improve.

Coaches do not seek the limelight. When you are working with someone to improve their performance you are preparing them for success, perhaps even fame. You will not be doing it to earn fame for yourself. A person who needs to be the centre of attention is unlikely to flourish in such a role.

# 3

# WHO CAN BE COACHED?

*As with potential coaches, there is a wide variety in potential coachees. This chapter explores those people who are more or less likely to take to being coached and will take an initial look at tactics for dealing with different types of people.*

For the partnership between coach and coached to work there needs to be a good coach and a receptive coachee. (Sorry, I don't like this word, but I don't have a better shorthand. Continually writing 'person being coached' is tedious for both me and you.) If you are coaching someone, what would you be looking for in them and how would you cope if it wasn't there?

The first thing I'd look for is energy and commitment to the task. If this is missing, then they will almost certainly pay lip service to the improvements that you plan, but will not put in the time or effort required to improve.

The next thing I'd look for is an acceptance and understanding of your role as coach. If they do not understand how you'll be working together, or understand but do not accept, then the partnership will not work.

Having got these there are a number of lesser difficulties that might need addressing. These are best summed up by what might be said by the coachee.

'I really can't be bothered.' Probably the worst thing you can hear as a coach (apart from 'Your house has burnt to the ground and your insurance policy has lapsed', or other such gems). Coaching someone who will not put effort into their own improvement is a thankless and ultimately useless task. If you cannot turn this attitude around, then stop coaching them. They will not improve until their attitude does. The best tactic for working on their attitude is to set very short-term improvement targets that they agree to and then explain that you're only prepared to continue with the effort if they work, too. If they don't reach the targets, agree another set. Make sure that they are an improvement on the current level, but are also clearly achievable. If they do not reach these, then stop coaching them. You'll be wasting your time if you continue.

'I already knew that.' This response is often used by people who mean more than this. They mean that they knew this and therefore don't intend to act on the knowledge. To overcome this you need to explain that most insights that a coach offers come from the person being coached. Such things are often known but not acted upon. Once they show signs of acting upon their knowledge, then they can play the smart-ass and tell you that they know it. Until they start acting upon it no amount of knowledge will be of any use to them.

'Now is not the right time.' There are people who want to improve themselves tomorrow. For some, this might be quite genuine, now may not be the right time. For others, this prevarication is merely a way of avoiding the effort while still feeling good about the potential. It's your judgement call. Are you dealing with someone who would benefit from being left for a while and who could be helped at some point in the future, or are you dealing with someone who could benefit from a little pushing right now? If it's the latter, then be careful not to push too hard. Remember your role as coach is to move at a pace that suits the coachee. Pushing is fine, bullying or taking decisions on their behalf is not.

'What makes you so damned smart?' You may well come across people who resent the whole notion of being coached. They might not wish to be helped at all or they might have a very specific view of the qualities that they need in a coach. For some it may be less to do with the coaching than their need for a particular type of person. Whatever the reason, if you have talked this through with the person you are trying to coach and they are still unhappy with your role, then back away. You cannot force someone to be coached. At the heart of the role is the agreement between the two parties. If this agreement (explicit or implicit) is not there, then coaching cannot work.

'Wouldn't it be better if I …?' Then there's the person who has to gainsay every suggestion or strategy for improvement. While being somewhat tiresome, this can actually work to your advantage. If there is no good reason why their suggestion should not be used, then going with it will give them an increased sense of ownership. If there is a good reason why yours is better (and your ego is not a good enough reason!), then explaining this is useful and may well be enough to bring them round.

'No.' There will come a time when someone will just refuse point-blank to listen to a suggestion you have or accept a target for improvement. When this happens, and the negotiation and persuasion fail, then the first step is to change approach. Would a different method work? Would a lower target be more acceptable? If there can be no compromise or if no common ground is found, then you might have to cut your losses and back away from coaching this person. Accept that they will not be coached or find someone with whom they have more rapport.

'I'm bored with this, let's move on to something else.' Attention span is a critical factor in coaching. Developing someone takes time. Them developing themselves takes effort. Some people are not suited to commitment to a long-term goal. For such people you might have to focus more on short-term deliverables. Celebrate inter- mediate targets reached. Set end goals that are actually steps on the way to a much longer goal. Persevere with these individuals because they are the ones most likely to surprise themselves when they do have help in applying themselves over a long time.

'I'll never be good enough.' In any one's development there comes the long dark teatime of the soul (as Douglas Adams put it), where doubt creeps in. In fact, doubt rarely creeps in. It usually marches in with cymbals clanging, drums beating and trumpets blaring. Short-term targets are good in these circumstances. 'OK, I'm not going to convince you that you can reach our long-term target of X, but you can see that very soon we could reach Y. Let's go for that and worry about X later.'

'Sorry I wasn't concentrating.' There are any number of excuses that someone will make to themselves for not achieving a target. To some extent, as coach, these excuses are irrelevant to you. You needn't care whether there's reality in them. If someone is cheating themselves they are cheating themselves, not you. This is their development, not yours. If they fail and excuse themselves for this failure, then just agree another target and work towards that. Obviously, if the failure continues you need to look at your approach and/or their commitment.

'Yes, I will. Sorry, I didn't.' Then there are those circumstances where current failure is excused by future performance. I will be doing better. I will work harder. I won't make that mistake again. Very often this is true. They will do better. They will work harder. They won't make that mistake again. Sometimes, this is just an excuse to get you off their back. If this is true, then either you or they have misunderstood your role. You are coaching their performance, not your own. Any failure to meet targets is their doing. They have no need to make excuses or promises to you. A clarification of your role would help, as would a clarification of their role in agreeing targets.

'But I want it NOW!' And finally, those people who can't wait for the improvement to materialize. You develop and agree a set of targets that will take them from where they are to where they want to be, and they then want to shortcut the process to get the results immediately. An approach that might work in these circumstances is to agree to a slightly more demanding set of targets and then to monitor progress against it. If they are committed enough to develop themselves to meet these targets, then they may well get results faster than you had originally planned. If they do not meet these earlier targets, then discuss with them about going back to your original plan.

Obviously, these example issues are just that. They are examples. They do not cover the entire gamut of issues that you'll hit when coaching. Nor could they ever. Hopefully, they will give you a notion of the role and the ways to develop it with the coachee. As your experience develops, so will your ability to handle situations not listed here.

# 4

# A COACHING MODEL

*It is often easier to grasp a subject if it is fitted within a model. This chapter lays coaching out within the acronym ADAPT: Assess current performance, Develop a plan, Act on the plan, Progress check, Tell and ask.*

In coaching someone you want them to adapt their performance. For this reason I have developed a simple model with the acronym ADAPT.

**A** – Assess current performance
**D** – Develop a plan
**A** – Act on the plan
**P** – Progress check
**T** – Tell and ask

OK, some of these are a little forced to create the acronym, but the model itself is sound.

*Assess current performance.* Before you can sensibly discuss an improvement in someone's performance you must assess for yourself where they are right now. With a sports person who competes as an individual, the level is relatively easy to assess – merely look at their records and statistics. With a team player it is more difficult, and then in a business context it becomes more difficult still. Even when a level has been established there is more to do. You need to understand for yourself how they achieve their current level. What style do they use? What tactics and strategies do they use? Where are they most comfortable? Where are they least comfortable? Now all of this obviously means that the performance being improved must be measurable. In business life many aspects of performance seem unmeasurable. They are not. In my experience, it is always possible to find a measure in one form or another if you are determined to do so. At times these might be crude approximations. At times they will be subjective. But they are there.

*Develop a plan.* The first stage of developing a plan to improve performance is to set the target for the performance level to be reached. How big an improvement does the coachee want? How big an improvement do you feel they can manage? Over what timescale could they achieve this improvement? The next stage is to break this target down into manageable time chunks. How far could you get in time X? How far in time Y? Finally, how far in time Z? At this stage keep the timescales short and the targets tightly focused. If necessary, make a plan that gets only part way to the ultimate goal. Keep this goal in mind, but do not be obsessive about planning for it. The next stage is to work on strategies for achieving this performance. Some may involve tuition, some may involve the coach observing and commenting on or questioning style, technique or approach. Some may involve observing experts in the area being coached. Some may involve the coachee observing their performance in some way – feedback from others, audio tape, videotape or some other form of self-observation. Finally, this plan needs to be formally agreed to by the coachee. They will have been involved in its development, but there is something about the act of saying, 'Yes, I agree to these targets and this plan' that gives a level of formality that somehow improves commitment.

*Act on the plan.* In some ways, although this is the part that most people see when they observe coaching, this is the easy bit. OK, there is skill and some difficulty in observing and commenting upon performance or questioning another's performance in a way that focuses on the things they need to change. But most of this stage is about turning up and doing what is needed to get from one stage of the plan to the next.

*Progress check.* This is obviously not one stage but a range of stages. Progress must be checked at each milestone, but should also be checked on the way to the milestones so that failing to hit a target should never be a surprise. Ideally, something can be done to improve the trend before the failure occurs. The progress check returns us to the point made earlier about the performance being measurable. If the measures used are imperfect, then the rigidity with which they are applied needs to be relaxed. Don't be tempted to treat a subjective measure as a scientific benchmark.

*Tell and ask.* This name of this section is the one that I'm least happy with. It is about discussion of progress against performance measures and discussion of any future improvement desired (which will take us straight back to the start of the process). This meant that I put 'tell' at the start of the title for the sake of the ADAPT mnemonic. It is obvious that asking needs to be first in reality, but ADAPA is less memorable! Discussion is at the heart of coaching. The coach needs to understand the motivation of the coachee, needs to understand their performance and needs to understand how to question them in order to draw from them ways of improving their performance.

Once this model has been worked through, and the coachee has improved their performance, you must decide between the two of you whether it is time to start the whole process over again. If you let it, the role of the coach can be a never-ending one.

# 5

# ACTUALLY DOING IT

*This final introductory chapter explains how the rest of the book works and how to put the coaching model into practice.*

The next section of the book actually forms the bulk of it. As with the rest of the *Instant* series, this is a section of around 70 one-page exercises that focus on specific aspects of the coaching task. These may be commonly encountered problems, tactics or strategies to use or exercises simply to put you or the coachee into the right frame of mind. By their nature, they are quick to start. Some may involve long periods of time in actually making them happen, but even these will be structured in such a way that you can undertake some elements of them instantly. Usually they will be quick and easy. Many of the exercises involve writing down thoughts or discussions. Whether you choose to do the writing or not is up to you. The advantages of following the advice and writing things down are that it formalizes thinking, structures the output and provides a record for later retrieval and reference. The major disadvantage is that it can seem like overkill or overformality, particularly at the start of the coaching relationship where many of these activities are focused. As with any aspect of coaching, use your own judgement and work in the way that suits you best.

This book is aimed at all coaches. Some will work in business, alongside the person or people they are coaching, some will work in other organizations, some will be personal coaches who offer their services to people with whom they have no day-to-day contact. There will be some exercises that this last group will find more difficult. Measurement of performance is a particular issue when you have no opportunity to observe that performance first-hand. At times, you might be coaching people who are ready to undersell themselves and so their assessment of progress is poor. At other times, you might be coaching people who are ready to oversell themselves and a similar danger arises. What is needed is some mechanism for a more objective observation of performance. For some activities, straight measurement will do. An obvious example here is athletics coaching, where a measurement of times or distances achieved is a good indicator of progress. At other times, you might need to work with the coachee to involve another in their measurement. I need to stress here that there is no question of lack of trust. You are working with the coachee for their benefit. Coachees will be the people that you work with. They will be the ones that you talk to. They are not the most objective observers of their own performance. If you are in the position of being unable to observe performance directly, then read the exercises with this in the back of your mind. Take whatever steps are needed to rectify this.

The previous chapters form a necessary support for the exercises. They have provided an understanding of coaching. The exercises should work on their implementation. In particular, the ADAPT model is at the heart of much of what you are about to read. It is assumed in many of the exercises and explicitly referred to in others.

**6**

# THE
# EXERCISES

*This chapter contains around 70 exercises, each approximately 350 words long, each self-contained, but building up to provide a total coaching package. Some exercises are aimed at specific areas of need while others are more general. The exercises are practical and short, ready for use whenever there is a spare moment or when the need arises. In the appendix at the back of the book, you will find lists of the exercises sorted by the star ratings at the end of each exercise. These lists may help you to find the sorts of exercises you require.*

# 6.1 | *Aiming high enough*

---

**Preparation** A knowledge of best in class performance for target
**Applicability** Any and every coaching situation
**Time taken** Five minutes (much longer if discussion results)
**Where/when** Anywhere convenient, at an early stage in the process

---

A key element of the coaching process is the objective or target that you are pushing towards. As you will have read earlier under the 'Develop a plan' part of the ADAPT model, the first step in developing a plan is to set a target. How do you know that the target is stretching enough? It is a waste to push hard for something that doesn't stretch the individual or team you are coaching. Similarly, it is demoralizing to set a target that is unachievable.

The secret here is to set the target in conjunction with the person or team you are coaching. If you feel that they have reasons or limiting beliefs that will cause them to set a low target, then you must play the role of challenger and conscience. At the end of the day you can only set a target that they will agree to willingly. If they feel bullied into it, then you have failed before you start.

A useful process in setting targets for people who limit themselves is to look at the best in class. Who is the best they know in the area you are trying to set as a target? In the world of sport, this is simple because records are public knowledge. In the world of business, the reliance will be on personal experience. Having established the best, and what the target would be if it were them here, it is then necessary to ask what shortfall on this target is acceptable. Starting at the best and working downwards is a better approach to making dreams come true than starting where you are and working upwards.

Personal coaching    ✪✪✪✪
Team coaching    ✪✪✪
Applicability to business    ✪✪✪✪
Development of you    ✪
Fun    ✪

## 6.2 | *Appraisals*

**Preparation** None (for the quick exercise)
**Applicability** Coaching related to a formal appraisal process
**Time taken** Five minutes (for the quick exercise)
**Where/when** How about right now?

Every large business and many small businesses have appraisal interviews. For me they are almost universally awful. This is not because they have to be. It is because they are often seen as a step in the salary review process rather than a tool in a coaching process. This exercise is about planning and carrying out an appraisal interview from a coaching perspective.

The first step is to make the meetings frequent. If your company only requires them annually, and many do, arrange your own intermediate ones so that you hold them monthly or quarterly. The second step is to have clear objectives. If you don't have these at the moment, then the first appraisal meeting that you hold should be a target-setting one. The next step is to prepare for the first meeting. In preparation you will need to have the information to hand that will allow a discussion of performance against target. It is useful to have examples of any behavioural aspects of performance. The final step is obviously the appraisal meeting itself. This is not about boss/subordinate. This is about coaching. The approach and the outcomes that you personally desire will make this successful or not. Are you genuinely approaching this from the perspective of the person on the receiving end of your attention? If not, then think about how you could change. Also think about whether a coaching relationship is genuinely applicable here.

If it is then this is a quick exercise that you can carry out straight away. Plan out the steps above. When will the meetings happen? What data do you need to collect? What will be the content of the first meeting? This exercise should be completed for everyone you are coaching and will take less than five minutes each. The resulting meetings will of course take much longer!

| | |
|---|---|
| Personal coaching | ✪✪✪ |
| Team coaching | ✪✪ |
| Applicability to business | ✪✪✪✪ |
| Development of you | ✪ |
| Fun | ✪ |

## 6.3 | **Backing off**

---

**Preparation** None
**Applicability** Whenever you question your role
**Time taken** Less than five minutes
**Where/when** Any time

---

In many coaching relationships there comes a time when you find yourself taking on the role of taskmaster. You are pushing, cajoling, even bullying the person being coached. This is far from ideal. Your role is to agree a set of targets and then to act as conscience, questioner and guide.

If you find yourself bullying or cajoling, then you need to ask yourself whether it is time to back off. A good quick check for this is the ICE scale. Mark from 1–10 the following:

   I  – Ideas: I have ideas that will help me to be more of a coach in this role
   C  – Coaching: I am operating in a coaching role
   E  – Enjoyment: I am enjoying what I am doing

A low Coaching score will determine whether or not you need to look at introducing new ideas. Obviously, if you are operating successfully as a coach then you do not necessarily need more ideas – though if you have them, why not give them a go? A low Enjoyment score (whether you are operating as a coach or not) will indicate that something is wrong with your role. A high Enjoyment score combined with a low Coaching score implies that you are not enjoying being a coach – again, question your role. A low score on all measures indicates that it is time to back off and give yourself and the coachee some space. If you are reluctant to do this, you could read through the book and see whether this generates any ideas that will bring your Ideas score higher.

| | |
|---|---|
| Personal coaching | ✪✪✪✪ |
| Team coaching | ✪✪✪✪ |
| Applicability to business | ✪✪✪✪ |
| Development of you | ✪✪✪ |
| Fun | ✪ |

# 6.4 | *Being realistic*

**Preparation** Needs to be done with the coachee
**Applicability** Any coaching situation
**Time taken** Half an hour
**Where/when** At the start of the coaching period

This exercise is about target setting. There is nothing more demotivating than an unachievable target. Making sure that the targets you agree are realistic is fundamental.

Targets are, by their nature, future based. How far into the future will depend upon the type of target being set and the area within which you are coaching. It is advisable to start by thinking as far ahead as you and the coachee can envisage. Ideally, try to think of an end state. Where do you want to get to? Then break the time between now and this end state into a few (say five) time periods. In order to achieve the target in period five, what would you need to have achieved in period four? In order to achieve the target in period four, what would you need to have achieved in period three? And so on.

Now look at the first period. If your end state is a long way away you might need to break period one into a few sub-periods. Then look at the first of these. Is what you are agreeing as a target for this period or sub-period realistic? Is it possible that this will be achieved? If not, is it possible to push harder on any of the other targets? Be aware at this stage that it is very easy to set yourself relaxed targets at the start and end-load the effort in a way that makes the targets for the later periods impossible. This is why it is advisable to work backwards in time rather than forwards. If you cannot realistically push the later targets, then the solution to making this realistic is to reduce the final target.

| | |
|---|---|
| Personal coaching | ✪✪✪✪ |
| Team coaching | ✪✪✪✪ |
| Applicability to business | ✪✪✪✪ |
| Development of you | ✪ |
| Fun | ✪ |

# 6.5 | *Being unrealistic*

---

**Preparation** Needs to be done with the coachee
**Applicability** Any coaching situation
**Time taken** Two hours
**Where/when** At the start of the coaching period

---

Coaching is about making dreams come true. There is nothing realistic about this. The previous exercise was very much done with feet on the ground and with realism in mind. This one is about dreaming.

Give the coachee a pile of magazines – a wide range with lots of images. Ask them to forget about the area you are coaching and to go through the magazines looking for and tearing out any images that appeal to them. Once they have a pile of these, ask them to make a collage of their dream. What would they really love to achieve? Use only the torn-out images. Having done this, ask them to write a short summary of their dream.

Now work with them to set a target that would achieve this dream. The next stage of this exercise is to go through the previous one about being realistic. Break the whole target down into time periods and say what would need to be achieved in each period. Is this possible?

If you are being unrealistic in your dreams, then it is likely that you have what appears to be an impossible target. The solution to this is to agree realistic targets and dream targets. If you are being realistic you will achieve this in the time period. If you are working towards your dreams you will achieve this. If you have two sets of targets for every period, it is likely that the person or team being coached will achieve more than a realistic target and they may or may not achieve the dream target. Whether they do or not, you are now able to demonstrate how much better they are doing than realistic targets alone would allow.

Personal coaching          ✪✪✪✪
Team coaching              ✪✪✪✪
Applicability to business  ✪✪✪✪
Development of you         ✪
Fun                       ✪✪✪

# 6.6 | *Building relationships*

**Preparation** None
**Applicability** Any time you want to think about relationships
**Time taken** 10 minutes
**Where/when** A short while into the coaching relationship

A coach is in a position of trust and potential power. If they are performing their role properly, then they may have a large influence on an individual or a team. In some instances this influence extends well beyond the area being coached.

This power and influence cannot be taken. Those being coached give it. They will not do this unless you have a strong relationship with them. Building relationships is not something that you will truly learn from an exercise like this. If you can't do this easily, then the coaching role is not for you. This exercise is intended more as a memory jog and checklist. Write down for yourself answers to the following questions.

How much do you know about the person being coached (or all of them individually if you are coaching a team)? What do you know of their likes, dislikes, hopes, dreams and desires? What do you know of their family and private lives? Where do they live? When is their birthday? Would they appreciate a card from you? Have you socialized outside the coaching situation? What do they think of you? What would they think of you in an ideal world?

There is no problem in being unable to answer any of these questions. Some coaching roles call for a closer relationship than others. If you do have problems answering them and you feel that you should not, then work on rectifying the situation. Remember, also, that it is not necessary to be loved to be a coach. It is necessary to have respect and trust.

I reiterate what I said earlier. If you do not build relationships easily, then no checklist will solve this for you. You must question whether you should be in a coaching role. If you feel that you should, then limit yourself to those coaching roles that do not need close relationships.

| | |
|---|---|
| Personal coaching | ✪✪✪✪ |
| Team coaching | ✪✪✪✪ |
| Applicability to business | ✪✪✪✪ |
| Development of you | ✪✪✪ |
| Fun | ✪✪ |

# 6.7 | *Catch them doing it right*

**Preparation** None
**Applicability** All coaching situations
**Time taken** A few days elapsed time
**Where/when** With your coachee and some work on your own

A piece of advice I was given more years ago than I care to remember was, 'Catch them doing it right'. At the time it flew in the face of most management thinking, which was about spotting the errors and correcting them. Traditional thinking was about catching them doing it wrong and putting that right. The advice I was given assumed a number of things. First, that people fundamentally want to do a good job. Second, that they sometimes need help to understand what doing a good job looks like. Third, that praise is a far more powerful weapon than criticism. Put these together and you come up with a philosophy that says that if you catch people doing it right and let them know that, then they will remember it and will strive even harder next time. Indeed, as a management style, this is very akin to coaching. As a coaching style, it is almost axiomatic.

So, what are you going to do about this? Here's an exercise that you might want to try that will take a few days, but it is well worth persevering with. For the next few days – or for the next few days of contact time with your coachee(s) – keep a record of the number of times you manage to catch them doing something right and the number of times you manage to catch them doing something wrong. The very nature of the exercise means that you will tend towards catching them doing it right rather than wrong. While you are doing this, notice how your style of coaching changes with each attitude. At the end of the few days, sit down by yourself and think through how well you are able to focus on the positive rather than the negative. Think through how well your coachee(s) responded. Think through how you felt about this style. If your feelings were generally positive, then you might want to build this into your toolkit as a regular activity.

| | |
|---|---|
| Personal coaching | ✪✪✪✪ |
| Team coaching | ✪✪✪✪ |
| Applicability to business | ✪✪✪✪ |
| Development of you | ✪✪✪✪ |
| Fun | ✪✪✪ |

# 6.8 | *Checking for understanding*

**Preparation** Needs to be done with the coachee
**Applicability** Any time there is a potential misunderstanding
**Time taken** A few minutes
**Where/when** Whenever needed as often as needed

Good communication is a key to success in the coaching role. If you are misunderstood or if you misunderstand you can undermine huge amounts of good work or, even, misdirect effort into the wrong areas. It is essential that you check regularly for understanding.

One useful tip is to get the coachee to summarize, in writing, their own understanding of long-term and short-term targets and immediate work under way to achieve them. This will allow you to see that these areas have not been misunderstood.

Where you feel that there is a breakdown in communication this short exercise may prove useful. It may feel somewhat false to both you and the coachee, but do try it out anyhow. It has been most useful to me.

Say what you are trying to have understood. Ask the person being coached to play back to you their understanding of what you have said. If what they say does not tally exactly with what you want them to have heard, then reiterate in different words and ask for a playback. Only when you are completely satisfied with their repetition can you move on.

This can of course be a two-way process. If you are not sure that you are understanding what they are saying, then you can play back to them what they have said and ask them to confirm that you have an exact understanding.

Sometimes, misunderstanding occurs because of associations that someone makes to an initial idea. If you feel that this might be causing a problem, then ask for a playback but also ask for them to spell out the consequences of what you are saying. This can often uncover some interesting misconceptions about intention or motivation. Again, this form of playback can be two-way.

| | |
|---|---|
| Personal coaching | ✪✪✪✪ |
| Team coaching | ✪✪ |
| Applicability to business | ✪✪✪✪ |
| Development of you | ✪✪✪ |
| Fun | ✪✪ |

# 6.9 Checking your coachfulness

**Preparation** Exercise 6.3, *Backing off*
**Applicability** All coaches
**Time taken** A few hours
**Where/when** Any time you can ask you coachees

Exercise 6.3, *Backing off* uses a quick test on scales of 1–10 to look at how your coaching is going right now. This is a solo exercise and is intended to reveal only what you think. There are times when you may want to ask those being coached how well you are performing for them. A simple series of statements with 1–10 scores can be very revealing about this. You can make up your own or you could use some or all of the questions below.

> X is a good coach
> X is trustworthy
> X is reliable
> I like X
> You know where you stand with X
> I feel that X is the right coach for me
> X will help me to achieve realistic targets
> X will help me to make my dreams come true

Then you might want a really risky open question such as, 'X would be a better coach if...'

Keep the list of questions short. This is a quick exercise and should not take you long to prepare and should certainly not take others a long time to respond to.

The most important thing to bear in mind about this sort of questionnaire is that without anonymity the type of answers you get will depend upon the type of relationships you have. In many coaching situations anonymity is difficult to achieve. If people love you, then they will not want to hurt your feelings. If they are scared of you, then they will not want to cross you. They are most likely to be honest when they respect and trust you and genuinely want to help you to improve.

| | |
|---|---|
| Personal coaching | ✪ |
| Team coaching | ✪ |
| Applicability to business | ✪✪✪✪ |
| Development of you | ✪✪✪✪ |
| Fun | ✪ |

## 6.10 *Coaching as an organizational norm*

**Preparation** Prepare and circulate a questionnaire (or fill in solo)
**Applicability** Any organization
**Time taken** Many days if widespread, a few minutes if solo
**Where/when** Any time

I think that coaching is a great way of developing, leading and managing others within an organization. I think that it would be wonderful if the leaders of all organizations saw themselves as coaches rather than as managers. I think it would be great if coaching was a norm in most organizations.

No quick exercise offered in a book like this can turn around your business, but it would certainly be possible for you to ascertain where your business stands by asking a few questions of yourself and/or others.

It would be possible for you to make this into an organization-wide questionnaire, but before you do that ask yourself how much value you would add to the data that you could collect by asking a few people. If you do ask others, make sure that you don't only ask those close to you as they may well have more understanding of where you are coming from than others. However, you might decide that you do not need the opinions of others and simply answer the questions for yourself. The sorts of questions that you might want to answer (using as answers strongly disagree, disagree, neither agree nor disagree, agree, strongly agree) could be:

I understand what coaching is.
I understand the benefits of coaching.
People around here understand what coaching is.
People around here understand the benefits of coaching.
Leaders of this business are trained as coaches.
Leaders of this business perform well as coaches.
Others in this business perform well as coaches.
I have targets for my own performance.
I am coached to help me to achieve my targets.
As a business we perform better than our competitors. (Substitute a more appropriate question for use in non-competitive organizations.)
Coaching is an organizational norm.

| | |
|---|---|
| Personal coaching | ✪ |
| Team coaching | ✪ |
| Applicability to business | ✪✪✪✪ |
| Development of you | ✪✪ |
| Fun | ✪✪ |

# 6.11 | *Coaching outside work*

---

**Preparation** None
**Applicability** Any time you want to extend your coaching
**Time taken** 10 minutes
**Where/when** Any time

---

The bulk of this book is written from a business perspective. It is written for use by those in businesses who want to improve their coaching performance. The opportunities to coach do not end at the end of the working day. There are many more situations where the skills of coaching are applicable.

Should you want to develop your coaching skills outside work, then it is useful for you to have in mind those situations where coaching might be a useful skill. This short exercise allows you to think that through and then take it a step further.

Ask yourself which of your current pastimes or activities you could bring coaching skills to bear on. Would those with whom you are involved welcome this or reject it? Which pastimes or activities that you are not currently involved in, but might become involved in, could you bring coaching skills to bear on? For instance, could you get involved with the local tiddlywinks team? Do you have any friends (close friends!) that you could offer some informal coaching, to help them to achieve a dream? Are there any members of your family that you could offer some coaching, to help them to achieve a dream? Finally, can you think of any other situation that might present opportunities for coaching?

Once you have drawn up this list, go through it and think about where you would enjoy getting involved and where you would not. Then go through again and think about where others would enjoy you getting involved and where they would not. Finally, think through how you would offer yourself as a coach in whichever area or areas you decide to progress.

Remember, the coaching relationship is explicit and open. It is not one that you slip into while others are not looking or that you do in an undercover or hidden way. Whichever of these areas you decide to progress, you must get the agreement and cooperation of those to be coached.

| | |
|---|---|
| Personal coaching | ✪ |
| Team coaching | ✪ |
| Applicability to business | ✪ |
| Development of you | ✪✪✪✪ |
| Fun | ✪✪✪ |

# 6.12 | *Coaching with others*

**Preparation** None
**Applicability** Any situation where you coach with another
**Time taken** An hour for the first meeting and regular bits thereafter
**Where/when** At the start and then regularly thereafter

The underlying assumption throughout most of this book is that you are acting as a sole coach. This is the most common and the easiest way of working. There are circumstances, though, where you may need or want to work in conjunction with someone else. This can have advantages in terms of two heads being better than one, in terms of support and in terms of companionship. It has disadvantages and the biggest of these is communication.

When you are coaching with someone else, you need to ensure that they know everything you know about the coaching situation and that they are thinking in the same way as you about the future development of those being coached. This is pretty much impossible to do fully so your objective must be to share as much as you can.

The two of you need an initial meeting. Sit down and agree a few ground rules. Are you going to share responsibility or does one person lead and the other act as support? Is your role the same for everyone being coached or does one of you take the lead with some and the other with others? How will you develop and share progress on targets? How will you develop and share progress on methods used to improve?

You then need to share information regularly. You will have agreed the *what* and some of the *how* on this. You have to make sure that you schedule time to make this possible and then stick to it. Updating one another is vital to your success as a team. Give it the time it needs.

| Personal coaching | ✪ |
| Team coaching | ✪✪✪ |
| Applicability to business | ✪✪✪✪ |
| Development of you | ✪ |
| Fun | ✪✪ |

# 6.13 | *Coaching your boss*

**Preparation** None
**Applicability** Where your boss has a performance shortfall
**Time taken** Half an hour to prepare for a meeting
**Where/when** In advance of suggesting this to your boss

The assumption elsewhere in this book is that you either have the explicit role of coach in a particular situation, or that you are a leader of others who is acting as a coach to them to improve their performance. If you are coaching your boss, then this assumption does not hold.

You will want to get involved in coaching your boss when their performance in a particular area falls down and this affects you in some way. You might also want to get involved in this out of a sense of altruism where their shortfall in performance does not affect you. There are two ways of approaching this. The best (in my opinion) is to be open and honest with them and to offer your services as a coach. The other is to be less explicit and to take on the role of coach without agreeing that openly. The second of these is risky.

Whichever you decide upon, you need to agree targets in some way and then to question, probe and monitor performance against targets on a regular basis. This is where the risk of trying to do this less explicitly comes in. Can you imagine how it will feel to your boss to have regular meetings with you at which you question them about their performance if you haven't agreed the role?

As a quick exercise to prepare for this role, write down for yourself the area that you wish to coach your boss. What is their area of performance shortfall? How does this affect you? How could you sell to them the idea of you coaching them? Anticipate their reaction and think through counters to any problems you might come across. Then go and meet the boss!

| | |
|---|---|
| Personal coaching | ✪✪✪✪ |
| Team coaching | ✪ |
| Applicability to business | ✪✪✪✪ |
| Development of you | ✪ |
| Fun | ✪✪ |

# 6.14 | *Coaching your peers*

**Preparation** None
**Applicability** Where your peers would benefit
**Time taken** Half an hour to prepare for a meeting
**Where/when** In advance of suggesting this to your peers

If they understand the coaching role, then your peers are much easier to coach than your boss. If they don't understand the role and yet you feel you could be useful to them, then the first thing that you need to do is to educate them about the role and its advantages. Below I have scored this exercise as a team coaching one on the assumption that you are coaching your peers as a group. If this is not the case, then you may either be coaching only one of your peers or coaching a group of them as individuals.

However you decide to approach this, then the exercise that you start with will be much the same as the one for the boss. There will, however, be a greater likelihood that you are doing this solely for their benefit and not because an aspect of their behaviour impinges on your role. This may not be true, but if you are coaching them solely for your own benefit, then you need to be absolutely explicit with them about your motivation. The coach's role is based on trust, not manipulation.

So, write down for yourself the level of understanding that you feel your peers have of coaching. If it's low, then how will you educate them? Now what area would they be most likely to want to develop? What is their area of performance shortfall? How does this affect the business? How could you sell to them the idea of you coaching them? Anticipate their reaction and think through counters to any problems you might come across. Then go meet them! Yup, I told you it was similar.

| | |
|---|---|
| Personal coaching | ✪ |
| Team coaching | ✪✪✪✪ |
| Applicability to business | ✪✪✪✪ |
| Development of you | ✪ |
| Fun | ✪✪ |

# 6.15 | *Coaching yourself*

**Preparation** None
**Applicability** Any time you want to improve an aspect of yourself
**Time taken** Two hours
**Where/when** As soon as you're ready

It is possible to act as coach to yourself. Taking on this role requires a great deal of self-exposure and honesty and some of us are not ready to be this candid with ourselves. If you feel that you are, then read on. You need also to be prepared to do a lot of writing down – when you have only yourself as a sounding board you need a written record.

Decide on a specific area that you wish to coach yourself. Write this down at the head of a sheet of paper. Now write down for yourself all of the ways that you have really succeeded in this area over the past year. Don't be shy about this and don't try to rush it. This is an exercise that is worth spending time on.

Next, write down all of the ways that you have not done so well in the last year. In what ways have you fallen short of your goals or your expectations? In what ways have you let yourself down?

Now think about how you would like to do in the year ahead. What would be different? What would you not do? What would you do more of or do for the first time? Write this down.

Finally, you need to think through your goals. What goals would you set yourself over a long time period? Now break this down into a few (say five) smaller time periods. What would need to be in place in the penultimate time period so as to achieve your goal? Now work back through each one answering that question. If your first period is more than a couple of months, then break that one down again. If your subsidiary goals feel unrealistic then you can either decide to change them or to work miracles. Don't just dismiss this last comment as flippancy. You may find that you can work miracles if you want to enough.

| | |
|---|---|
| Personal coaching | ✪✪✪✪ |
| Team coaching | ✪ |
| Applicability to business | ✪✪ |
| Development of you | ✪✪✪✪ |
| Fun | ✪✪✪ |

# 6.16 | *Delegation*

**Preparation** None
**Applicability** Any boss with tasks to delegate
**Time taken** An hour initially and then as long as the task
**Where/when** Any time

I have been a manager in my time. I've even been a leader in my time. I know that delegation can be a tough thing to do. The reasons are usually that you choose to delegate the things that are important to you and thereby take a significant risk on someone else's ability, or to delegate the trivia and thereby undermine those to whom you delegate.

One way of delegating the significant stuff without taking such a risk is to use delegation as a coaching opportunity. First, think through the things that you do and decide which you do not personally need to be involved with. Second, look at the significance of each item and try to find a few significant tasks and a few trivial tasks that you can delegate. The reason I'd suggest this is that delegating all of the significant stuff leaves you with all of the trivia. Finally, talk to the person to whom you're delegating.

For this to work well you need to be explicit with them about the reasons for doing this and your expectations of them. As with all coaching, very specific targets, ideally within tight time boxes, are essential.

The key difference between coaching and delegation is that the negotiation of the targets is tighter when delegating. If you are coaching someone for personal development and they wish to take a leisurely path then, as their coach, you can question and challenge but the decision is theirs. If you are delegating and the person to whom you are delegating wants to take a leisurely path, then the chances are that you can't afford to delegate to them.

Now is the time for monitoring performance against targets and correcting any shortfalls. If the targets are being missed by a long way, then you will either have to help in a more active way or take back the task. The bottom line is that this form of delegation is a genuine win–win if it is working, but if it is not then the buck stops with you.

| Personal coaching | ✪✪✪✪ |
| Team coaching | ✪✪ |
| Applicability to business | ✪✪✪✪ |
| Development of you | ✪✪✪ |
| Fun | ✪✪✪ |

# 6.17 | *Developing the right environment*

**Preparation** None
**Applicability** Anyone that coaches in a single location
**Time taken** Half an hour
**Where/when** Whenever you choose

Whether you work in a business, work for a non-profit organization or work on your own, the environment within which you coach can have a marked impact upon your effectiveness.

The ideal environment to create is a relaxed, homely one that puts you and your coachee at ease. This short exercise is intended to help you to think through how you might develop that.

First, think through and write notes for yourself about the sort of environment that makes you feel most comfortable. If this is too broad a question, then think through the differences between your workplace and home. What sort of furniture do you have in each place and what effect does that have upon you?

Next, think through the barriers that you have around you. By this I mean both physical and psychological barriers. Physical barriers would be desks, tables, walls, doors and partitioning. Psychological barriers would be things like secretaries that need to be bypassed, a forbidding approach or an environment that is markedly different to that which your coachee is used to. Make notes on these.

Finally, think through those things that you can change. What barriers can you remove – both physical and psychological. What furniture could you change? If this sounds like overkill for a coaching session, then ask yourself why you need these barriers or this furniture otherwise. Could you be more comfortable if they were removed? If their removal would make you less comfortable, can you leave them but make them less significant? Alternatively can you change your own needs so that you are more comfortable with fewer barriers?

| | |
|---|---|
| Personal coaching | ✪✪✪✪ |
| Team coaching | ✪✪ |
| Applicability to business | ✪✪✪✪ |
| Development of you | ✪✪✪ |
| Fun | ✪✪✪ |

# 6.18 | *Developing trust*

---

**Preparation** None
**Applicability** All coaches
**Time taken** Ongoing
**Where/when** Ongoing

---

I have mentioned a few times that trust is a key to the coaching role. It is worth building on this statement and talking a little about how trust can be developed.

Coaching is a participative process. It is not about the coach telling. It is not about the coachee doing as they are told. It is about discussion and questioning. For this to work well, both parties need to be able to communicate well with one another and need to have trust. The coachee needs to trust that the coach has their best intentions at heart and needs to trust in the coach's ability. The coach needs to trust that the coachee will do as they agree and will be honest about the results.

For the most part trust develops over time. To an extent it can be helped along. At the simplest level is the coachee's trust in your ability as a coach. It is fairly clear that if you continually apologize for your lack of experience or question your own judgement then you will undermine trust. It is useful to keep at the front of your mind that you need not give advice. If you question and play back effectively then you will find that the coachee advises themself. Using lots of phrases like, 'What I hear you say is …?' and, 'So it seems that you are suggesting that you …?' means that you have no need to question your judgement since you are merely acting as a sounding board. If this sounds like copping out, then you are taking too interventionist a view of the coach's role. Very often (though not always), the coach is just a sounding board.

The next level of trust is the personal one. You need to have established ground rules with your coachee about confidentiality and other minefield areas. You then need to stick to them religiously. Even a slight slip in this area is a major betrayal of trust. Guard against it. Beyond this their level of trust in you will depend upon how trustworthy you seem. There's little that a book like this can do for you if you come across as someone others wouldn't buy a used-car from.

| | |
|---|---|
| Personal coaching | ✪✪✪✪ |
| Team coaching | ✪✪✪ |
| Applicability to business | ✪✪✪ |
| Development of you | ✪✪✪✪ |
| Fun | ✪✪ |

# 6.19 | *Doing yourself out of a job*

**Preparation** Exercise 6.16, *Delegation*
**Applicability** Any manager
**Time taken** An hour or two for the initial exercise
**Where/when** As soon as you feel brave enough

This exercise is really an extension of exercise 6.16, *Delegation*. It stems from an odd personal belief of mine that the most successful people are those that strive continually to do themselves out of a job. If you don't subscribe to this notion, then it will seem counter-intuitive. How can you be successful if you are unemployed? In reality, those that are successful in doing themselves out of a job are almost always kept by their company because they are seen as successful and most smart companies want to hang onto the successful. If your company isn't this smart, then do you really want to work with them? I guess I should point out at this stage that this approach has always worked for me, but that I accept no liability for any loss of income or employment caused by following my advice.

As with the delegation exercise, break your job down into sub-tasks. Which ones do you feel that others are able to do immediately? Which ones do you feel that others could do with some development? Are there any tasks you do that no one else can do? If so, then you are in a very dangerous position. Yes, you are secure in your present role, but you can never change role or move on because you can't hand this task over to anyone. Now is the time to start planning ways to do this.

Assuming that there are no tasks that cannot be done by someone else, then you need to draw up a plan to hand over everything you do to someone else. An alternative is that you talk this over with your boss and point out how you could save them some cost – yours.

| | |
|---|---|
| Personal coaching | ✪ |
| Team coaching | ✪ |
| Applicability to business | ✪✪✪✪ |
| Development of you | ✪✪✪✪ |
| Fun | ✪✪✪ |

# 6.20 | *Eliminate the negative*

**Preparation** Read 6.50, *Positive visualization*
**Applicability** Wherever the coachee hits a bad patch
**Time taken** A few minutes to a few days
**Where/when** As soon as things start to go wrong

When coaching someone, there will come a stage in their development where nothing goes right. If it can screw up, it will screw up. If they can miss a target, they will miss a target. This is a dangerous time because it is the time when they are most likely to give up or to make a stupid decision on the basis of a short-term difficulty. As the coach, this is the time when your questions need to be very specific and very pointed. You might even need to become directive.

The first thing to focus on is the period before this when the world was not so black and when things worked. Try to establish in the coachee's mind how they felt then and how they feel now. Try to focus on the positive feeling and use that as a springboard for moving forwards. Get them to record with you the successes that they have had and to talk through how they made them come about. Was there something different about their attitude, their approach, their lifestyle, or is it just that they're being unlucky right now.

Next, you need to work with them on visualizing success. There is nothing more powerful than a dream that you believe in. If you can reignite their belief in their dream, then you can help them to step towards success once more. See exercise 6.50, *Positive visualization*, for more on this.

Finally, one thing that you as the coach will need to consider is whether their current targets are realistic. If they are missing targets it could be that things are just screwing up for them right now. It could also be that between you, you have managed to set unrealistic targets. This is an area for personal reflection. You should only discuss this with the coachee once you are convinced that this may be a factor.

| | |
|---|---|
| Personal coaching | ✪✪✪✪ |
| Team coaching | ✪✪ |
| Applicability to business | ✪✪✪ |
| Development of you | ✪ |
| Fun | ✪✪ |

# 6.21 | *Emergencies*

**Preparation** Anticipation during planning
**Applicability** All coaching situations
**Time taken** Ongoing
**Where/when** As and when emergencies arise

For the most part, coaching is an ordered and planned way of working. It is about creating targets with someone, and you will help them to achieve these by observing and questioning so that they and you can suggest ways of working better. There are times when the planning goes out of the window and things need to be dealt with now. It might even be that there is something that can't wait until your next planned session.

The sorts of things that might constitute an emergency will vary from organization to organization, individual to individual and role to role. Some examples might be an athlete injuring themselves, someone you are coaching in your business being offered another job, or a necessary resource being taken away at a critical time.

By their very nature, these sorts of emergencies will not form a part of your planning. Indeed, it is often difficult or impossible to have thought through contingencies in advance. For some items, this will be possible: at the start of the planning process, when agreeing targets, think through the resources and people that are necessary for a successful outcome. Are there alternatives available to any of these? How would you be able to make use of them and how might they affect the targets?

For those that are not foreseeable, you will have to be able to react on the spur of the moment. You will need to question the coachee about things that they can do to overcome the obstacle created, and to work with them on strategies and tactics for coping. Beyond this, and the use of your natural wit, there is little advice to offer. It happens – enjoy it.

| | |
|---|---|
| Personal coaching | ✪✪✪✪ |
| Team coaching | ✪✪✪✪ |
| Applicability to business | ✪✪✪✪ |
| Development of you | ✪✪✪ |
| Fun | ✪✪✪ |

# 6.22 | *Engendering belief*

---

**Preparation** Get hold of a roll of paper and lots of coloured pens
**Applicability** Any situation where a lack of belief is a block
**Time taken** One hour
**Where/when** Any time

---

There are a range of reasons why people need coaches. Sometimes they need someone to act as a conscience. Sometimes they need a sounding board. Often they need someone to help them to believe in themselves. If you feel that this last is the case, then this short exercise might prove useful.

Get hold of a huge piece of paper. I use wallpaper-lining paper because the roll is very long and gives plenty of space. Now get the coachee to write down in a thick coloured pen everything that their harshest critic would say they are bad at in the area being coached. Put lots of space between the items because you'll have a lot to write around them. When they think they've exhausted the list, push them harder. Make them really dig down to the bottom of the barrel.

Now, in a smaller and different coloured pen, get them to write next to each bad item the things that their biggest fan would say. Why has their critic misunderstood them? What mitigating circumstances exist? What are they good at in this area that compensates? Many people will need pushing and prompting in this area. If they do not believe in themselves, then they will have great difficulty imagining that they could even have a fan, let alone what the fan might say.

Finally, in yet another coloured pen, get them to write next to each bad item everything they could do to improve. What training could they undertake? What care could they take? What work will they choose to do to improve? Again, you might need to prompt and to offer suggestions here because if they found the solutions obvious they might well have done something about it.

Now, together read through and analyse the results that you will have laid out in front of you. Is there anything here that seems insurmountable? If so, is there any way to break it down into manageable chunks? For everything else, what would you like to build into your coaching targets? What are you willing to leave out for now?

| | |
|---|---|
| Personal coaching | ✪✪✪✪ |
| Team coaching | ✪✪ |
| Applicability to business | ✪✪✪✪ |
| Development of you | ✪ |
| Fun | ✪✪✪ |

# 6.23 | *Establishing pace*

---

**Preparation** None
**Applicability** Where you have an issue with the coachee's progress
**Time taken** As long as it takes
**Where/when** Whenever you can discuss this with them

---

When you are coaching someone, the pace at which they do things can well determine progress. You will work with people who want everything to happen now and so will smash at obstacles like a bull in a china shop. You will work with people who will be happy to wait for the tomorrow that never comes.

Sometimes, you will want to slow people down. It might be that they are not learning lessons they need to learn because they are pushing too fast. It might be that they are cutting corners and achieving their targets at the expense of some level of quality that you haven't been monitoring.

Sometimes, you will want to speed people up. It might be that they are doing themselves a disservice by taking longer than they need over everything. It might be that they are being painstakingly meticulous about things that need not be focused upon.

In general, the way to change their pace is to establish the root cause of the issue and to focus on that. It is rare that you will be able to say that they are going too fast or too slow and that this will be enough. If they are cutting corners, then discuss other quality measures with them. If they are focusing on unnecessary detail, then discuss the bigger picture.

Very often they will understand for themselves where the root cause of their pace issue lies. If they do not, then you will need to probe to help them to uncover it. Generally, it is a bad idea for you to form an opinion about this and to offer it as a solution. Try to uncover a solution jointly.

As a last point, be prepared to accept that the issue with their pace might be your problem. If they are happy with the results they are producing and the rate they are moving, then you might choose to back off.

| | |
|---|---|
| Personal coaching | ✪✪✪✪ |
| Team coaching | ✪✪ |
| Applicability to business | ✪✪✪✪ |
| Development of you | ✪ |
| Fun | ✪ |

# 6.24 | *Establishing the two-way process*

**Preparation** None
**Applicability** Any coaching relationship
**Time taken** Half an hour
**Where/when** Early in a coaching relationship (or now if not established) initially alone and then with the coachee

You will have gathered by now that my view of coaching is intensely personal, or even interpersonal. It is about you as the coach interacting very closely with one or more people who are being coached. This is not about you making yourself available to them to be used as they will. This is a two-way process. You need to establish this very early in your relationship.

One swift way of doing this at the outset is to have, as part of your preliminary meeting with the coachee, a discussion about rights and responsibilities. What are you offering as coach? What will you expect from the coachee? Similarly, what are they offering and what can they expect from you? It is a good idea to record this discussion and to make sure that you both have a copy. Obviously, where the coaching is team-based, each member of the team needs a similar understanding.

A quick exercise that you can do now in preparation for this is to write down for yourself what you feel you might be offering a coachee. What are you prepared to do and what are you not prepared to do? What will you need from them in return? What is the minimum level of commitment that you can expect? Obviously, unless you have a particular coaching relationship in mind this exercise is theoretical, but there will be general principles that will apply to pretty much any coaching relationship you establish. If you are having trouble knowing what you would ask of a coachee, try this exercise from the other perspective. What would you ask for if you were being coached? If you became absurdly demanding, what would you want? Looking at these demands, where would you as the coach want to set the limits?

| | |
|---|---|
| Personal coaching | ✪✪✪✪ |
| Team coaching | ✪✪✪✪ |
| Applicability to business | ✪✪✪✪ |
| Development of you | ✪✪✪ |
| Fun | ✪✪ |

# 6.25 | *Following up*

---

**Preparation** Understanding what you need to know from the coachee
**Applicability** Any coaching relationship
**Time taken** Half an hour to an hour for planning, plus an hour for the chat
**Where/when** At the end of the coaching relationship

---

Very often when you establish a coaching relationship it will be with a specific goal in mind. Your preparation, your focus and your activity will be on helping the coachee to achieve that goal. So, when you get there the relationship finishes, does it? Possibly it does, but it may not. It might be that the goal you helped them to achieve was a milestone and that more lie ahead of them. It might be that you could help with these. It might be that achieving the goal has created a vacuum and that they would appreciate help with establishing a new course. Whatever the situation, it is always worth establishing a means of checking whether your involvement really has finished.

When you establish the initial plan with the coachee, include within it a follow-up session that occurs after everything else has finished. Ensure that enough time will have elapsed for them (and you) to have reflected upon the relationship and to have thought through whether any benefits might arise from continuing it. If the coachee sees no value in this, ask them to humour you and to build it in anyway. If your coaching relationship is one where you charge for your time, then offer this session for free. Just ensure that it happens.

To plan for this follow up session now, think about what you would include. What feedback would you seek about the relationship? What sorts of feedback would you want to give? A useful rule of thumb here is that feedback should never be a surprise. So if you are planning to give feedback at the follow-up session, then it should be in areas that you've covered in the actual coaching sessions Overall, plan what messages you would like to take away and what messages you would like to give the coachee. If the relationship looks set to continue, do not do too much planning at this meeting, schedule another session for that.

Personal coaching    ✪✪✪✪
Team coaching    ✪✪✪
Applicability to business    ✪✪✪✪
Development of you    ✪✪✪
Fun    ✪✪✪

# 6.26 | *From why to how*

**Preparation** None
**Applicability** Every coaching relationship
**Time taken** Half an hour for the exercise; during the whole relationship
**Where/when** Before coaching, then apply while coaching

A mantra to keep in your head while coaching is, 'Why, then how'. Your initial questions and observations will be focused upon why a particular behaviour or activity is happening. Why are they not achieving their full potential? Why is that next step in progress eluding them? Why, why, why? Much of your value as a coach will be in extracting these *why* observations from the coachee. This is only the first phase of the mantra. The next is the one where the progress happens.

Having established the *why* we need to move on to the *how*. How can we take a step forward from here? How can we add an extra step to the progress? How can we stretch beyond this current limit? Here again, remember that your role is not necessarily to suggest solutions. You are extracting the *how* from the coachee. They are likely to have a better view of how they can progress than you.

Separating the *why* from the *how* provides a useful mechanism for ensuring that you have observed and questioned current behaviour and performance before leaping into solutions. It is a way of preventing you from applying stock solutions to every issue.

An exercise that you might find useful as a step in developing this mindset is to review a recent coaching relationship. If you have not coached, then think of a time that you were coached. If you have not been coached, then think of any time that you have made a step forward in progress. Review this period and ask a series of why questions. Why were you/they not progressing? Why were you/they setting limits upon performance? Why, why, why? Then go through and review the how. How did you/they move on from there? How did the performance shift? How, how, how?

| Personal coaching | ✪✪✪✪ |
| Team coaching | ✪✪✪✪ |
| Applicability to business | ✪✪✪✪ |
| Development of you | ✪✪✪ |
| Fun | ✪✪ |

# 6.27 | *Getting beneath anxiety*

**Preparation** None
**Applicability** Any time you feel your coachee might be anxious
**Time taken** An hour
**Where/when** Alone for practice; with the coachee for real

There are times when the person that you are coaching will be anxious. There are whole ranges of causes for this anxiety. Some of them will be associated with the coaching process and some of them with the field being coached.

Generally, those associated with the coaching process will be addressed by discussing what you will be doing, how you will be going about it and by being open to any questions that the coachee may have. Those anxieties associated with the field being coached are harder to deal with here because the approach that you take will depend upon the cause of the anxiety. Often that cause is not obvious because the anxiety itself may reflect something that is not known even by the coachee. I'm not suggesting that you set yourself up as a psychoanalyst, but you will have to be very empathetic and may have to spend time digging beneath the surface to uncover what's going on and the reasons behind it.

One way to practise this is to deal with your own anxieties. You may have some about the whole coaching process. Take a few moments to write these down now. Once you have done that look at the first one and ask why it is an area of concern. Write down the answer(s). Now look at them and ask in turn why they might be. Write down the answers. Keep on asking why until you reach a point where the answers seem trivial or unhelpful. Now move on to the next concern, and so on. Once you have completed this, look at the whole list and hunt within it for the underlying fears that drive the anxieties you may feel. This may not be obvious, but dig in there because finding them can make a significant shift. If this process works for you, then you might try it with your coachee.

| | |
|---|---|
| Personal coaching | ✪✪✪✪ |
| Team coaching | ✪✪ |
| Applicability to business | ✪✪✪✪ |
| Development of you | ✪✪✪ |
| Fun | ✪✪ |

# 6.28 | *Giving feedback*

**Preparation** None
**Applicability** All coaching situations
**Time taken** Half an hour to prepare; as long as it takes to do
**Where/when** Now

I said earlier that feedback should never be a surprise. This would be a good place to expand on that notion. The first thing to say is that in the coaching relationship feedback is a way of life. It is happening all of the time and is two-way. Feedback can take the form of a casual observation, a thought-through, longer discussion or a formal session. It is always done from a position of trust and even love. It is never an opportunity to dump on the coachee. The bottom line is that it is happening all of the time.

Part of the feedback process is signalling areas of concern soon enough that when they become issues neither you nor the coachee are surprised. When they form part of the discussion the attitude will be that this was expected.

To prepare yourself for giving feedback, sit down and list those areas that you feel need to be discussed. Decide how big each is. For the smaller ones, make a decision to talk about them informally sometime. For the larger ones, schedule time with the coachee to discuss them explicitly. From now on this needs to be the way that you work. Any issue that you become aware of needs to be raised. As you become aware of it, note it down and decide what is the most appropriate form of feedback. Schedule time to make this happen.

When scheduling time, remember that there are two sorts of feedback. There's the stuff we all like where we get praised, and there's the stuff that few of us like where we get to hear some of our faults. Do not mix the two. If you give bad feedback followed by good the recipient gets so mired in the bad that they don't hear the good. If you give good feedback followed by bad the earlier stuff is discounted as sweetening the pill. As a friend of mine said to me years ago, 'Everything before the "but" is bullshit'.

| | |
|---|---|
| Personal coaching | ✪✪✪✪ |
| Team coaching | ✪✪✪✪ |
| Applicability to business | ✪✪✪✪ |
| Development of you | ✪✪ |
| Fun | ✪✪ |

# 6.29 | *Goal setting*

---

**Preparation** Create time and space for the discussion needed
**Applicability** Every coaching situation
**Time taken** An hour or more
**Where/when** At the start of the coaching relationship

---

In the next section we'll talk about goals, but before we do it is important to talk about the process of setting them. Setting goals is, ideally, something that the coachee should do for themselves. They will know what they want to achieve and the time frame in which they want this. Where it works well, the goal-setting process is merely a formalization of this. The role of the coach is to prompt, challenge, question and then to record the desired goals. There are times when this does not work. Generally, this is when the coachee's aspirations are way below those that the coach believes they could achieve. This gives you, as a coach, something of a dilemma. A goal that the coachee does not buy into is worse than useless. They will not work to achieve it and then, when they do not, the only possible feedback is that they have failed. So, they must be willing to accept a goal, even if they believe it will be a real stretch for them.

One way of approaching this is for the coach to suggest short-term stretch targets that will challenge the coachee but, because of their short-term nature, do not involve an impossibly high stretch. A coordinated series of such targets can result in a long-term target that the coachee would have thought impossible if they had been presented with it at the start of the process.

When setting goals, make sure that you have plenty of time and that there is nothing that will distract your or the coachee's attention. Make sure that every goal is agreed and recorded. You keep a copy and give a copy to the coachee. From now on your role is to help them to achieve this.

| | |
|---|---|
| Personal coaching | ✪✪✪✪ |
| Team coaching | ✪✪✪✪ |
| Applicability to business | ✪✪✪✪ |
| Development of you | ✪✪ |
| Fun | ✪✪ |

# 6.30 | *Goals*

**Preparation** Collect together any goals you have previously set
**Applicability** All coaching situations
**Time taken** Half an hour for review
**Where/when** Whenever you are able

Goals are at the heart of the coaching process. They are the yardstick against which the coachee measures their performance. Often, they are simple to set, sometimes the nature of the task makes them harder.

Most goals need to be time-bounded. You know when they are due. Some goals cannot be strictly limited by time because they are moving into territory where predicting progress is impossible. For these, the next suggestion is most important.

Goals must have a measurable achievement. You and the coachee must know what success looks like and must know when that success has been achieved.

Goals must be stretching. They should not be something that you know you can do at the outset. Indeed, a 50 per cent chance of failure is a measure that I often use.

Goals must be achievable. This is a direct contradiction to the previous suggestion, except that the 50 per cent chance of failure also assumes a 50 per cent chance of success. Less than this is unrealistic.

Goals drive a step-change in performance. If the goal you are setting does not move the coachee a long way forward why are you bothering? Step-change is always something to aim for. In some fields, and at some levels of performance, it will be impossible, but always have this in the back of your mind.

Goals can be discarded. This sounds like a negative, but the important point here is that once you have achieved a goal you should throw it away and not have it lingering around in the background. If you set measurable, tangible goals then they will be discardable. If you do not, then they might well not be. You might choose to discard a goal when it is achieved and replace it with one that is the same but with a higher level of performance. This is fine.

Now, spend some time reviewing goals that you have set recently for coachees (assuming that you have any at the moment), and decide whether they meet these criteria. If they do not, then question yourself hard about why. Is it because the goal is wrong or because these rules do not apply for some reason? Be honest with yourself.

| | |
|---|---|
| Personal coaching | ✪✪✪✪ |
| Team coaching | ✪✪✪✪ |
| Applicability to business | ✪✪✪✪ |
| Development of you | ✪✪✪ |
| Fun | ✪✪ |

## 6.31 | *Going the extra mile*

---

**Preparation** None
**Applicability** Particularly where you coach multiple coachees
**Time taken** Half an hour or less
**Where/when** Any time

---

At times, as a coach, you will need to push the coachee quite hard. At times they will push themselves quite hard. Guard against falling into the trap that poor sports coaches sometimes do – shouting at and berating their coachees. People perform from fear very poorly and only for a short time. They respond far better to love. This sounds horribly soft and fluffy, but often this is what coaching is about. Going the extra mile applies to you every bit as much as it does to the coachee. One of the huge drawbacks of adopting a coaching role is that it is demanding of your time, it is demanding of your attention and it is demanding of your emotional commitment.

Giving your all to the coachee(s) can be extremely draining and so you need to establish some limits for yourself.

Sit down with a pad of paper and a pen and answer the following questions.

1. Are there any times that you are not prepared to deal with a coachee? Some people set aside specific coaching sessions, some do not. Whatever you do, what are your limits?
2. Are there specific places that you are not prepared to deal with the coachee?
3. If you set specific session times with them, are you prepared to overrun?
4. Are you prepared to help them with issues that fall outside the area you are coaching?

If your answers to these questions are universally expansive – you are prepared to give hugely of yourself – you need to question what protection you have to guard against coaching taking over your life. If your answers are extremely restrictive – you give of yourself only at prescribed times and in prescribed places – you might need to question whether you are really going the extra mile on behalf of the coachee.

| | |
|---|---|
| Personal coaching | ✪✪✪ |
| Team coaching | ✪✪✪ |
| Applicability to business | ✪✪✪ |
| Development of you | ✪✪✪✪ |
| Fun | ✪✪ |

# 6.32 | *'I can't do it'*

**Preparation** None
**Applicability** Whenever the coachee has hit a block in progress
**Time taken** At least an hour, probably much more
**Where/when** In conjunction with the coachee

You will get to a stage in the relationship with your coachee where you are convinced that they can achieve a goal that they are convinced they cannot. You need to turn around their thinking. It is as Henry Ford used to say, 'Whether you believe you can or whether you believe you can't, you're absolutely right'. So, how do you turn around thinking when someone has convinced themself that they cannot do something?

The first step is probably to explore with the coachee the source of their limiting belief. How do they know that they can't? Is this limit the result of something that has been said to them, something they know about themself, something that they know about the world or simply something they know to be true? Having explored this, you might want to look at the fear that lies beneath the assumption they are making. Any limit that we place upon ourselves stems from an underlying fear. Uncovering this can be a useful trigger to progress. Are they scared of failing? Are they scared of succeeding? Are they scared of letting someone down (including themself or maybe even you)? What is it that drives the limit? Often, when you feel you have uncovered such a fear it is useful to probe deeper because the first fear that springs to mind may not be the one that lies the deepest. Once you are satisfied that you have reached an underlying fear that is driving their limit, you need to work on it to overcome its effect. The best way that I have found of doing this is to use positive affirmations (see 6.49, *Positive affirmations*). Some feel that such affirmations are merely wishful thinking, but I can assure you from personal experience that they are wonderful at turning around a limiting belief or its underlying fear.

| | |
|---|---|
| Personal coaching | ✪✪✪✪ |
| Team coaching | ✪✪ |
| Applicability to business | ✪✪✪✪ |
| Development of you | ✪ |
| Fun | ✪ |

# 6.33 | *'If only they wouldn't...'*

**Preparation** None
**Applicability** Any time the activity of others limits the coachee
**Time taken** Well over an hour – possibly weeks
**Where/when** With the coachee, as soon as the problem is identified

'I could do so much better if only they wouldn't ..., ..., ...' – fill in the blanks. Almost everybody has somebody to blame for aspects of themself. Almost everybody can point to an aspect of their performance and say that it would be better if others would behave differently. So what? It really doesn't matter at all. The world is the way the world is and you have two choices – accept it or change it. Moaning about it does no good whatsoever.

The person or people that you are coaching will, at some point in this process, point to others as the source of their shortfall or as a limit that holds them back. You need to work with them on the accept-it-or-change-it principle to get them to the point where they move on from this.

The first step is to establish with the coachee how real is the limit that they are imposing upon themself. Are they really being held back by the behaviour of others or are they just using them as a scapegoat? Having established this, the next step is to work out ways of changing any behaviour in others that is limiting performance. What influence can the coachee bring to bear? Will talking with the others be enough? If not, what other tactics could they use? The next step is to see ways that the coachee could change their own behaviour, so that whatever is causing the limit no longer has an effect. Could they work elsewhere, in different ways or at different times? Could they develop another aspect for a while and come back to this? The final step is when there is still something that others are doing that limits performance and there is nothing that can be done to modify that or ameliorate its effects. At this stage you need to work with the coachee on ways to live with the limit.

In an ideal world we would not allow others to adversely affect our performance in any way. In the real world they do. The bottom line is always to accept this or change it.

| | |
|---|---|
| Personal coaching | ✪✪✪✪ |
| Team coaching | ✪✪✪✪ |
| Applicability to business | ✪✪✪✪ |
| Development of you | ✪✪✪ |
| Fun | ✪✪ |

# 6.34 | *Individual coaching*

**Preparation** Exercise 6.31, *Going the extra mile*
**Applicability** All individual coaching situations
**Time taken** An hour or so
**Where/when** Before the relationship starts or as a review now

There are some significant differences between coaching an individual and coaching a team. When coaching an individual, there are a number of things that you need to think through and to be aware of. What is your current relationship with them? If you have no relationship with them, and they have come to you purely as a coach, this is all to the good because you have no modification of your or their behaviour to make. If you are currently a colleague of theirs, then for the coaching to work well they need to understand that you will be strict about rules of confidentiality. If you are currently their boss, then you need to be able to establish a more equal relationship for coaching to work. Similarly (but more challengingly), if they are your boss, then you will need to establish equality at least while the coaching is taking place.

Once the tone of the relationship is established (and this may take some time), you also need to establish the ground rules. This is best done alone initially, thinking through what you want from this relationship, and then in discussion with your coachee. We have discussed in 6.31, *Going the extra mile*, the times that you will be prepared to spend with the coachee. If you haven't done this exercise, then do it now. You will also need to think through the type of relationship that you want to have with the coachee. How dependent upon you are they likely to become? How dependent upon you are you prepared to let them become? In general, dependency in a coaching relationship can be great for the coach's ego, but awful for the development of the coachee. It is best avoided. Sit down for a while by yourself thinking through how this relationship will work and then spend some time with the coachee agreeing the ground rules. If you coach different people regularly, then you only need do the thinking once (since your requirements are unlikely to change from person to person), but then hold the discussion with each individual.

| | |
|---|---|
| Personal coaching | ✪✪✪✪ |
| Team coaching | ✪ |
| Applicability to business | ✪✪✪✪ |
| Development of you | ✪✪✪ |
| Fun | ✪ |

## 6.35 | *Killing fear*

---

**Preparation** None
**Applicability** Any individual coaching relationship
**Time taken** About two hours
**Where/when** With the coachee, in private

---

Fear is an insidious beast. It lurks at some depth beneath every one of the limits we place on ourselves. It is tricky to identify it (because even your coachee will probably not know what the driving fears are), but essential if you are to be successful as a coach.

Ask the coachee to list with you the things that they have done in the last year that have disappointed them or at which they have felt they haven't excelled. Take time over this because this list will be useful. Now, with them, go through the list and ask them how they have contributed to their disappointments. What contribution have they made to things not working their way? Make this a separate list. Now, what effect have others had on their disappointments? Who has let them down or held them back and in what ways? This is yet another list. Then looking through all of the lists, work with the coachee to establish a list of their beliefs about the world. What do these lists indicate that they believe about themself, the situations they have been in and the effects of others? This is yet another list. Now the final part, and one of the most probing, is for you to probe their beliefs to try to uncover the fears that lie beneath them. This isn't for you to tell them what their fears are. This is a journey of personal discovery. By all means help them but, finally, it has to be them that agrees to any fear you list. A useful way of probing is to ask them why they believe something to be so and then continue to ask why for any answer that they give.

Once you have a list of fears you have some material to work with. The way that you work with this will depend hugely on you, the coachee, your relationship, the fears uncovered and the goals that you have. It isn't possible for me to say here and now how this will work. Back to your skill and your intuition!

| | |
|---|---|
| Personal coaching | ✪✪✪✪ |
| Team coaching | ✪ |
| Applicability to business | ✪✪✪✪ |
| Development of you | ✪✪✪ |
| Fun | ✪✪ |

# 6.36 | *Knowing what you know*

**Preparation** None
**Applicability** All coaching relationships
**Time taken** An hour
**Where/when** Any time

It has always fascinated me that in sports some of the very best coaches never made the top of their sport. Olympic coaches are not necessarily ex-Olympic athletes. A coach can coach a number of events even where they have only competed in one. Some of the best coaches are not athletes at all. So how can they be so smart that they can pass on this knowledge without apparently possessing it? The answer should be no surprise. They are not passing on knowledge, they are uncovering it. They are not being smart about the event; they are being smart about coaching. Having said that, it is obvious that the coach does need to know a great deal about the discipline they are coaching; they just don't need to know more than the coachee does. What they need to know is how to draw the best out of the coachee.

On your own, sit down and list for yourself the areas that apply to a particular coaching relationship where your knowledge excels that of the coachee. Now write down the areas where their knowledge excels yours. Having done this, think through the future relationship and think through what aspects of your knowledge it is necessary to pass on for them to succeed. Now think through what aspects of their knowledge it is necessary to bring to the fore. Are there likely to be obstacles in the way of this? If so, then list them and decide now what approaches you'll make to overcome them.

If you have found that you have a long list of things that you need to pass on to them for them to succeed, and if this list is made up of items of knowledge specific to their goals, then you need to think hard about whether you are truly going to be coaching. Might a straight teaching relationship work better? If, on the other hand, you have very little knowledge to contribute, then you need to think through how you will talk to them about the coaching relationship. They will need to know what you are offering and what you are not.

| | |
|---|---|
| Personal coaching | ✪✪✪✪ |
| Team coaching | ✪✪✪ |
| Applicability to business | ✪✪✪✪ |
| Development of you | ✪✪✪ |
| Fun | ✪✪ |

# 6.37 | Learning and learning styles

**Preparation** None
**Applicability** Primarily individual coaching situations
**Time taken** An hour, sometimes longer
**Where/when** Wherever you and the coachee will be comfortable

Different people have different ways of absorbing information from the world around them. Understanding how your coachee learns and what differences there may between their style and your own could be of crucial importance to establishing your relationship.

Sit down with your coachee and work through the following questions (if you are coaching a team this exercise may be less applicable or else you may decide to treat them as a collection of individuals). Remember that the answers may not be absolutely either/or. Some people are able to cope with a range of styles.

What is their action bias? If they are action-oriented, then they will be better at absorbing information by doing rather than studying or being told. If they are less action-oriented, then studying would be a better approach.

How visual or verbal are they? Some people need to see images associated with their learning while others need words. What is their bias? Do they prefer to read about something or watch a video?

At what times of day do they best absorb information? Some people's brains perform best in the morning, others in the afternoon, others in the evening. There may well be combinations of best times. Mine, for instance are morning and evening. The afternoons are relatively poor times for me to be doing anything that requires a brain.

Once you have jointly established how your coachee learns you might want to turn the tables and do this for yourself. Now, between you, look at any differences there may be and discuss what impact these are likely to have on the way you work together. Having done that you could start to plan your approach on the basis of this. Remember that this information is merely a guide. If there are other factors that affect, for instance, the times of day that you work on something, then don't allow this material to dominate.

| | |
|---|---|
| Personal coaching | ✪✪✪✪ |
| Team coaching | ✪ |
| Applicability to business | ✪✪✪✪ |
| Development of you | ✪ |
| Fun | ✪✪ |

# 6.38 | *Learning to believe*

**Preparation** None
**Applicability** Wherever you feel that the coachee won't make it
**Time taken** An hour
**Where/when** Whenever it's needed

Faith can move mountains, we're told. Well, you don't have to move a mountain, you just have to move someone else's performance. Indeed, you don't even need to do that. You just have to give them the tools to help them to move their performance. One of the most fundamental tools is belief. If they believe in their own ability and believe that they can do what is required, then they will have a far higher chance of success than if they don't. Give them that belief and half of your job is done.

OK, so how do you do that? And the answer, as always, is that it depends. It depends, first, on how much you believe in their ability. It is truly tough to convince someone of something when you are not convinced yourself. An early question then is: how can you believe in them? If you have coached a number of people and have seen them make dramatic shifts in their performance, then it is easier to believe in a dramatic shift in this coachee. If there is another obstacle in the way of your belief, then you need to work on that.

Sit down and list out scores on a scale of 1–10 for the following attributes. Your scores will indicate how these will help the coachee to succeed. A score of 1 indicates that it's a no-hoper and 10 indicates that no work is needed in this area.

1. Their current skill level.
2. Their mental attitude.
3. Their commitment to success.
4. The time they have available.
5. Their belief in you as a coach.

Having scored these attributes, you will have a much better idea of why you do not believe in their success. You should understand what is causing your lack of belief. How can you work on this? If it is about time, how can you persuade the coachee to dedicate more? If it is about mental attitude, how can you motivate them? Once you get to this stage you are no longer dealing with your belief in the coachee. You are dealing with your belief in yourself as a coach. Work on the tactics you need to follow and convince yourself that you can coach them through this. Now convince them.

| | |
|---|---|
| Personal coaching | ✪✪✪✪ |
| Team coaching | ✪✪ |
| Applicability to business | ✪✪✪✪ |
| Development of you | ✪✪✪✪ |
| Fun | ✪✪ |

# 6.39 | *Lecturing and hectoring*

**Preparation** None
**Applicability** All coaches
**Time taken** A few days elapsed with an hour's review
**Where/when** As soon as you wish to start

Many people have seen the image of the coach shouting at the team at half-time so as to get them to lift their game. This can be satisfying for the coach, but it is demoralizing for the team and does nothing positive for performance. I know that there are many coaches who disagree with me. My belief is that whatever coaching situation you are in, lecturing or hectoring your coachee is counterproductive. Avoid it at all costs.

A useful way of establishing how much this approach is part of your style is to monitor yourself over a period of time and to note down what your approach has been.

How much time do you spend talking and how much do you spend listening? If you don't spend the vast majority of your time listening or observing, then you are probably too fond of the sound of your own voice and need to step back a little.

How much of your talking is with your voice raised and how much of it is quiet conversation? Except for those coaching in noisy environments, there should be very little of your time when you need to raise your voice. The only exception I can think of here is where you need to demonstrate passion about something. Doing this in a low voice can be counterproductive.

How much time do you spend telling and how much asking? In general, you should be uncovering the coachee's knowledge of ways to improve their performance. There are obviously exceptions to this where your role is more directive but these, I believe, move from coaching into teaching.

Having established your own answers to these questions (ideally from self-observation over time), you could now think about how you want your style to be. It is fine for you to disagree with me and to have a model of coaching that involves pushing hard against your coachees. What is not fine is that you are doing this unthinkingly. So, once you have thought about it, at least you have a basis on which to act.

| | |
|---|---|
| Personal coaching | ✪✪✪✪ |
| Team coaching | ✪✪✪✪ |
| Applicability to business | ✪✪✪✪ |
| Development of you | ✪✪✪✪ |
| Fun | ✪✪ |

# 6.40 | *Letting go of the solution*

**Preparation** None
**Applicability** Individual coaching, particularly around long-term life goals
**Time taken** Two hours
**Where/when** Anywhere private to work with the coachee

Coaching is very goal-oriented. This makes it very solution-based in many instances and this is not an issue. There are times, however, when focusing on a particular solution will move your coachee into an area where they don't want to be. What I mean here is that you and the coachee have a goal in mind. That goal is going to be quite specific in its aims. The reason the coachee has this goal is because they want to achieve something, improve something, change something or create something. There may come a time when that particular something for one reason or another becomes difficult to achieve. This does not mean that the coachee need fail in their achievement because they could still achieve something that delivered the same or better qualities than the original goal. Getting at the qualities that lie beneath a goal can be of fundamental importance in establishing what to aim at.

Sit down with your coachee and write down the goals that you agree. For each, probe why they want to achieve them. What is it about achieving this goal that will make them happy? What qualities will this achievement bring into their life? Having done this, group the qualities and jointly examine what else they could do that would deliver these qualities. You can afford to be as fanciful as you choose at this stage because these other achievements will not necessarily be ones you ever choose to aim at. Having established a range of possible achievements, ask your coachee to examine which they would want to set as goals now? It might well be the same ones as you started with. What is important is that you have examined others and have developed a notion of the qualities that underlie the solution. This will allow you to re-examine the solution later in the coaching relationship and check that it will still deliver the qualities, and also check whether there is an alternative solution that will deliver the qualities that would be easier to achieve.

| | |
|---|---|
| Personal coaching | ✪✪✪✪ |
| Team coaching | ✪ |
| Applicability to business | ✪✪✪✪ |
| Development of you | ✪✪ |
| Fun | ✪✪ |

# 6.41 | *Love*

---

**Preparation** None
**Applicability** All coaches
**Time taken** Half an hour to an hour
**Where/when** Wherever, whenever you choose

---

The trouble with love is that it is a word which carries a huge amount of emotional baggage for most people. The difficulty with using any other word is that nothing else conveys the passion that sits behind that one. So, what's love got to do with it? Well, what's love got to do with anything? I believe that it is a fundamental driving force. That everything we do stems from a basis of love or fear. The philosophy behind this would take too long to go into here, but I would urge you to take a look at the questions in this exercise if only to establish in your own mind what is driving you.

How well do you love yourself? This is a really tricky one to be honest about. Human beings are experts at lying to themselves about how they feel about themselves. If you find this a tough question, then let's break it down. First, how much do you love your body? Is it the body of your dreams? Does it do for you what you want it to? How much would you choose to change it if you could? Second, how much do you love your mind? What aspects of your thinking processes would you change if you could? Would you want a better memory? Would you want to be wittier? Would you want to think faster and respond quicker? Finally, how much do others love you? Are you inherently lovable? Every one of the changes you wish to make in yourself is an indicator of not loving yourself. True love is unconditional.

Having looked at how much you love yourself, the next thing to ask is how much do you love what you do? If you won the lottery tomorrow and no longer had to work, would you stop? Would you change what you do? What aspects of your life would remain unchanged and what aspects would you choose to alter?

The final question is how much do you love those you coach? This is very tricky territory because love has so many sexual connotations. It is possible to truly love others without there being a sexual relationship. Think about the coaching relationship and ask how much you base it on love.

Once you have been through this soul searching, and it can be pretty tough to do if you don't treat it glibly, you could ask yourself what would you like to change about yourself, what you do and your relationship with your coachees.

| | |
|---|---|
| Personal coaching | ✪ |
| Team coaching | ✪ |
| Applicability to business | ✪ |
| Development of you | ✪✪✪✪ |
| Fun | ✪ |

# 6.42 | *Marking time*

**Preparation** None
**Applicability** Whenever you hit a snag that inhibits achievement of a goal
**Time taken** Under an hour
**Where/when** As soon as you are aware that you've hit a snag

Time is one of the key dimensions that you have to deal with as a coach. It is also a key tool in your toolkit. Never underestimate the power of time scales in terms of targets. First, you have to have them. Without a timescale a target is not a target. Second, you can work with the form that they take. A very long-term goal becomes much more likely to be achieved when it is broken down into a series of very short-term goals. The long and the short of this is that whenever you hit a snag that looks like it will get in the way of achievement of a goal, one of the first things you should think about is how to manipulate time.

Assuming you have hit a snag, here are some questions that might well prove useful for you and your coachee to think through.

1. How important is the original deadline? If we change it, what knock-on effects might it have?
2. How much are we using time between now and the deadline? Could we fit more periods of activity into this time?
3. How are resources being used? Could we bring in more resources and crash the timescales?
4. What time are we misusing currently? Are there things that are being done that we could bypass or do without altogether?

Having considered these questions, you are in a strong position to change things for your coachee's advantage.

| | |
|---|---|
| Personal coaching | ✪✪✪✪ |
| Team coaching | ✪✪✪✪ |
| Applicability to business | ✪✪✪✪ |
| Development of you | ✪ |
| Fun | ✪✪ |

# 6.43 | *Measuring improvement*

---

**Preparation** None
**Applicability** All coaching relationships
**Time taken** Half and hour per coachee
**Where/when** Whenever

---

I cannot stress enough the importance of improvements in performance being obvious to the coachee. If they can't see progress they may well lose heart. They will certainly not move forward as well or as fast as they would if they can see progress. This is one reason why I always recommend breaking long-term goals down into a series of short-term ones. Progress becomes more obvious and the individual steps are smaller.

A corollary to this is that measurement is important. Having a goal that is measurable is necessary if you are to measure improvement. Even if the measure is subjective, it is better than nothing. Do, however, avoid subjective measures that depend on how the coachee feels. This will cause the measure of their performance to be a reflection of their mood and that can lead to a downward spiral when things start to go wrong.

As a quick exercise to see how successful your goals are on this scale, go through all of the goals you have for all of your coachees and ask yourself these questions.

How objective is the measure of performance? How much does opinion come into it and, if it does, whose opinion are we talking about? How directly is the measure related to success? Remember, there may be some measures that are indicators of something that you would like to measure but cannot. For instance, you might not be able to measure staff morale, but you could measure absence through sickness.

When will the coachee next have an indication of increase in performance? This is a tricky area to get right because the intervals need to be far enough apart to allow a real increase in performance, but close enough together to be motivating. How clear are you about what shortfall in performance would indicate something going wrong and what shortfall is acceptable as variation and noise?

How able are you to see the results (do you work alongside your coachee?), and how much must you rely on them reporting back to you?

While going through this you might want to be asking yourself which goals you would change to make them more successful as motivational measurers of performance. If you decide that something needs changing, you will need to talk this through with your coachee.

| | |
|---|---|
| Personal coaching | ✪✪✪✪ |
| Team coaching | ✪✪✪✪ |
| Applicability to business | ✪✪✪✪ |
| Development of you | ✪✪ |
| Fun | ✪✪ |

# 6.44 | *Mission*

---

**Preparation** None
**Applicability** Any team coaching
**Time taken** A few hours
**Where/when** As soon as you can create the time

---

A mission is a short statement that explains why a team exists. It is a useful tool for a team where the team will last longer than the goals you are setting. If the team exists only for the achievement of fixed goals, then the goals themselves can act as the mission. Even for long-term teams you may decide that a mission is superfluous. To develop a mission you will need the whole team together and a few hours for creating and refining ideas. It is useful for this meeting to be relaxed and informal. Answering some questions could kick off the initial development. None of these have a single answer. The more answers you collect for each the more material you have to work with. The sorts of questions that you might want to ask are: Why do we exist as a team? What are we here to achieve? What sort of hole would we leave if we ceased to exist?

Having done this you might want to get some passion into it by collecting passion words and applying them to the work of the team. I have done this in the past by asking people to talk about their favourite movies and to describe the passions that each movie arouses. Why does it matter to you? What do you feel while watching it? Another approach is to get the team to create a collage of pictures ripped from magazines. They should initially choose pictures that convey a feeling or passion associated with the team and that they find positive. Once the collage is created, collect words that describe it.

Having done all of this, get the team to use these inputs (the answers to the questions and the passion words) to describe the aims of the team with as much passion and verve as possible. From this, distil a pithy and motivating statement.

| | |
|---|---|
| Personal coaching | ✪ |
| Team coaching | ✪✪✪✪ |
| Applicability to business | ✪✪✪✪ |
| Development of you | ✪✪ |
| Fun | ✪✪ |

# 6.45 | *Now is all you can do*

---

**Preparation** None
**Applicability** All coaching relationships
**Time taken** An hour
**Where/when** Now

---

Think about yesterday. What did you do? Where were you? What were you feeling? Having done this for a few moments, ask yourself where yesterday exists. The answer is that it exists in your head as a memory. Now think about tomorrow. What plans do you have? Who are you seeing? What pressures will you have on you? Having thought about this ask, yourself where tomorrow is. It also exists only in your head. Even now, this very instant, you are receiving the world as sensory inputs and these are being interpreted inside your head. The present also is merely thought. The thing that makes now different from the past or the future is that you can act now. You can have an impact now. You can do things now. You cannot do anything in the past. It is gone. You cannot do anything in the future. You can plan for it, but by the time you can act then that future must be the present. The present is the only time you can do anything.

Coaching is by its very nature a future-oriented task. You are planning with the coachee for an improvement in the future. The only way that you can make this real is by acting now. This is an important concept for your coachee to grasp. If they are perpetually future-focused they will miss the levers that they have right now. If they are stuck in looking at past performance, they will miss the changes they can make to the future by the choices they can make now.

As a quick exercise, sit down with your coachee and ask them to draw a chart of the time between when you started working together and the achievement of their goal. Ask them now to draw a line on this chart that represents the level of effort they need to make. Now ask them to draw another line that represents the significance of this effort in the achievement of their goal. This should give an indication of where they feel their leverage is. Now is the time to have a discussion about the nature of time and the fact that the only point they can put in effort is now. The only point of any significance is now. They can plan for their effort and they can plan for significant events, but these plans are only conceptual. Reality is now. It is where effort needs to be.

| | |
|---|---|
| Personal coaching | ✪✪✪✪ |
| Team coaching | ✪✪✪ |
| Applicability to business | ✪✪✪✪ |
| Development of you | ✪✪ |
| Fun | ✪✪ |

# 6.46 | *'Now look what you've done'*

**Preparation** Exercise 6.43, *Measuring improvement*
**Applicability** All coaching
**Time taken** Half an hour for planning
**Where/when** Now

Earlier in 6.43, *Measuring improvement*, we talked about the importance of measures. They are important, but alone they are not enough. You also need constant feedback that reinforces any improvement. Whether you see your coachee every day, once a week or even coach by telephone sessions, you must always ensure that any improvements are referred to. Any work that has been done to move towards the goal needs to be mentioned. All steps that have been taken must be highlighted.

Have you thought about the structure of your coaching sessions? If not, then now might be a good time. There are a number of activities that you need to make sure you have covered, not in the way of a checklist or a clumsy move from one to another, but more in the way of a reminder at the back of your head.

Each coaching session needs to have a huge amount of listening. This is not an inactive task, it is very active and may need you to probe and question fairly vigorously. You will then need to structure what you have heard and play it back to the coachee in a way that highlights the moves towards their goal. Between you, you then need to plan activities for the period up until the next coaching session. If your coaching sessions also involve the activities for improvement (most often the case with sports coaching), then these things will be at the start of the session and the actual activities for improvement later.

Plan now the next coaching session you will hold. Think through how much time you need to give to each element of the session and how you will make it happen.

| | |
|---|---|
| Personal coaching | ✪✪✪✪ |
| Team coaching | ✪✪✪✪ |
| Applicability to business | ✪✪✪✪ |
| Development of you | ✪✪ |
| Fun | ✪✪ |

## 6.47 | *Overcoming a lifetime of learning*

**Preparation** None
**Applicability** New coaching relationships
**Time taken** Half an hour
**Where/when** Plan now, implement later

There are two things that I want to cover in this section. The first is your coachee's attitude to the coaching relationship and the second is the process by which they learn. These are closely linked.

To start with the first. It is likely that, when they first enter a coaching relationship with you, your coachee will have had no experience of coaching (this will not be true for most sportsmen or sportswomen). They may well be expecting you to teach them. The attitude of people new to coaching is often, 'OK, tell me what I need to learn to do next'. This is not your role and you will need to avoid being sucked into playing it. Almost everything that the coachee needs to learn will come from them. You may be able to add tools that help them or tips that move them in a certain direction, but the learning is theirs. This is counter to all of their previous experience.

The second point, which is very closely linked to the first, is that if a coachee has had a lifetime of learning from external sources they may not be good at listening to the learning that comes from themself. They are likely to attribute more weight to learning from a significant other than from themself. You may need regularly to play back to them what you hear them say. If you do this, be sure to stress that this is what they have said. This is not your wisdom it is theirs.

Give some thought now to tactics that you could bring to bear when faced with a new coachee who is not comfortable with a relationship that is not teacher–pupil based. What would you say to them? What difficulties are you likely to face? How would you deal with these? What difficulties are they likely to face? How can you help them through these?

| | |
|---|---|
| Personal coaching | ✪✪✪✪ |
| Team coaching | ✪✪✪✪ |
| Applicability to business | ✪✪✪✪ |
| Development of you | ✪✪ |
| Fun | ✪✪ |

# 6.48 | *Planning to coach*

**Preparation** None
**Applicability** Primarily to those starting out as coaches
**Time taken** An hour (longer if research is needed)
**Where/when** As soon as you can

If you are reading this book because you intend to get into coaching and you haven't yet started, there are a number of things that you might want to think through. Even if you are an experienced coach and you are reading this book as a refresher, you might want to review what you do by giving some though to the overview of your coaching.

Coaching is a broad field. Different people in different circumstances will approach it in different ways.

Take a little time now to review the following questions. The first question you will need to approach is: face to face or not? Generally, it is necessary to meet your coachee for an initial planning session, but for some types of coaching there need not be any more face-to-face meetings. The coaching can be conducted as telephone interviews, letter, e-mail, or Internet chat sessions. Which approach will suit the style of coaching and the discipline you plan for?

If you are to meet face to face, the next question is location. In general, do you plan to coach where your coachee is, where you are, or on neutral ground? If it is to be where the coachee is, before you say yes, you need to ensure that there is adequate privacy and that the atmosphere is conducive to this work. If it is to be on neutral ground, then you need to select a suitable venue and, if necessary, pay for it.

You also need to think about charging. If coaching is to be your livelihood, then you will need to establish what you can charge. This is determined by a whole range of factors. Who else is coaching in your area? What are they charging? What is your relative level of experience? What can people in your area afford? Most importantly, what value do you believe you can add to your coachees?

A final question is where are your clients coming from? How will they know about your services? How will they understand the value you can add? Why should they bother to contact you?

Having answered these questions, you should have a much clearer idea about what you are doing and why you are doing it.

| | |
|---|---|
| Personal coaching | ✪✪✪✪ |
| Team coaching | ✪✪✪ |
| Applicability to business | ✪✪ |
| Development of you | ✪✪✪✪ |
| Fun | ✪✪ |

## 6.49 | *Positive affirmations*

---

**Preparation** None
**Applicability** Any aspect of your life or your coachee's
**Time taken** An hour
**Where/when** Whenever you feel the need

---

Everything in your life is created by your thoughts. In part, they create the way you experience things and, in part, they create the things themselves. There are three actions involved in this creation – thought, word and deed. When you believe that something is so, or will be so, you will start to talk about it and then you will do something to bring it into your life. Positive affirmations start at the *word* part of this trilogy. They are statements about you or your world that change the thoughts and the deeds in the creative trilogy. This makes, 'I am' the most powerful statement in the universe. You saying, 'I am' in a particular way can genuinely change the way you are.

Try this short exercise for yourself to decide whether you wish to use it or adapt it to use with your coachees.

Think about some quality that you want in your life or want more of in your life. Write yourself a statement that starts with, 'I am', 'I have', 'I choose', or 'I desire' and build this quality into it. Now write that statement over and over. As you are writing, listen for the voice in your head that argues against this statement (it will be there, it always is!). Write down what it says. Now write another affirmation to counter this. Write this over and over again and listen for the voice. Continue until you get bored or the voice shuts up because it gets bored.

Repeating this exercise regularly really does allow you to create new realities in your life. If you want to find out more about this process, then read either *The Artist's Way* or *Creative Visualization* (see Chapter 7).

Personal coaching     ✪✪✪
Team coaching     ✪
Applicability to business   ✪✪
Development of you     ✪✪✪✪
Fun     ✪✪✪

# 6.50 | *Positive visualization*

---

**Preparation** None
**Applicability** Many situations in your life and your coachee's
**Time taken** An hour
**Where/when** With some privacy; any time you wish

---

At the end of the last exercise I mentioned the book *Positive Visualization* (see Chapter 7). This subject is so large that you should view this exercise as merely a taster and read that book. This exercise is only one type of visualization exercise. There are many, many more that you could learn and usefully employ.

Your subconscious mind deals with the world in symbols. This fact can be a very useful tool for talking to the subconscious and affecting the way that it sees the world and, thus, the limitations it places upon you. Think of something that limits you and the qualities you'd have in your life without it. Many people will think of money, some will think of other things. Now sit yourself down and relax. To do this breathe slowly and with each breath out imagine that you are breathing out tension. As you breathe out the tension, feel a different group of muscles in your body relaxing. Spend some time doing this. Now create in your mind the picture of a wooded glade. At one side of this glade is a cliff with a cave in it. On your back is a knapsack with your limit inside it. Leave this at the entrance to the cave and enter the cave. As you walk in you notice that the interior is warm and comfortable and surprisingly light. Ahead of you, you can hear the sound of running water. As you approach this sound you see a golden goblet that is overflowing with a crystal-clear liquid. This liquid is the qualities you wish to bring into your life. It is flowing from this goblet and spilling onto the floor. You drink from the goblet. As you drink you feel the qualities suffusing your being. Miraculously, as you drink, the goblet continues to fill and to overflow. It will never empty. There is an abundance of what you desire and this abundance will always be there for you. When you have drunk your fill, replace the goblet, knowing that you can return to it at any time. Make your way out of the cave into the dappled sunshine and slowly bring yourself back to wakefulness.

This sort of imagery and visualization can be extremely powerful when working with coachees. I urge you to try it and to find out more.

| | |
|---|---|
| Personal coaching | ✪✪✪ |
| Team coaching | ✪✪ |
| Applicability to business | ✪✪ |
| Development of you | ✪✪✪✪ |
| Fun | ✪✪✪✪ |

# 6.51 | *Problems, problems, problems*

**Preparation** Exercises 6.49, *Positive affirmations* and 6.50, *Positive visualization*
**Applicability** Whenever your coachee is stuck
**Time taken** From one hour upwards
**Where/when** Whenever your coachee is stuck

We've all heard the statement, 'Every problem is an opportunity', and many of us will have rejected it because of the trite philosophy that often supports such positive thinking. There is, however, a very deep truth in this statement that should not be rejected too swiftly. If you believe that you are beset by problems, then you will be beset by problems. If you believe that there are opportunities within them, then you will see the opportunities. Sometimes, though, this will take more than just repeating the 'Every problem is an opportunity' mantra. Your coachee, when beset by seemingly insurmountable obstacles, will not thank you for smiling inanely and repeating this to them over and over. This could be a good way of finding out how violent they are prepared to be!

If you have not yet done so, try the previous two exercises, 6.49, *Positive affirmations* and 6.50, *Positive visualization*. These provide useful tools for countering many problems and you might choose to use these as tools with your coachee.

There may be other things that you will need to do. An early one would be to try to uncover the source of the problems. To what extent is the coachee creating them, to what extent is it the environment and to what extent is it other people? Delving into the source will sometimes suggest to the coachee routes that they can take to move around or to overcome their problems.

Another thing that you could do is to work with the coachee on some creative solutions to the problems. Creativity techniques attack a problem by approaching it from an oblique angle; this often suggests approaches that you might otherwise have missed. There is not space in this book to cover this, but the book *Instant Creativity* (see Chapter 7) does this well.

Finally, develop, with the coachee, a short-term plan that will include some visualization and affirmation tools and the results of the creative thinking will help them to move forward.

| | |
|---|---|
| Personal coaching | ✪✪✪✪ |
| Team coaching | ✪✪✪ |
| Applicability to business | ✪✪✪✪ |
| Development of you | ✪✪ |
| Fun | ✪✪✪ |

# 6.52 | *Pushing and yielding*

---

**Preparation** None
**Applicability** All coaches
**Time taken** An hour
**Where/when** Whenever, wherever

---

Your relationship with your coachee will usually be one of mutual respect and cooperation. This brings about a high degree of equality. There will be times when you will need to push hard to move your coachee forward. There will be times when you will need to give way rather than create conflict. Knowing when and how these apply can be quite tricky. In general, this is a piece of intuition that you will learn with experience. Thinking through different scenarios may help you to short-circuit some of the experience this implies.

Think through conflicts that you have had with your coachee(s) in the recent past. If you are not currently coaching, then think of other life situations. Write down a sentence for each that reminds you of the situation. Now write down the point of conflict. Next, on a scale of 1–10, score how important you feel it was to the development of the coachee that you had this conflict. Now score on a scale of 1–10 the importance of resolving that conflict there and then. You will need to be brutally honest with yourself in completing this exercise because most of us after a conflict know that we were right to do what we did, even if a mountain of logic stands in the way of us knowing that.

Having completed this, think through situations where you avoided conflict. These can be hard to remember, but try to find a few. Write a sentence as a reminder and then write what the issue was that you chose not to confront. Score the importance of that issue to the coachee's development. Now score how well that issue has been resolved since the conflict was avoided.

This short exercise should give you a whole bundle of food for thought. First, you could think through those points of conflict that need not have arisen – either because they were not important enough for the coachee or because they could have been dealt with better later. Now you can look at those conflicts you have avoided. If they are unimportant to the coachee, then avoiding them was the right thing to do. If they have been resolved subsequently, then avoiding may well have been the right thing to do. If they are important issues and still outstanding, then you may need to push harder now to resolve them.

| | |
|---|---|
| Personal coaching | ✪✪✪ |
| Team coaching | ✪✪✪ |
| Applicability to business | ✪✪✪ |
| Development of you | ✪✪✪✪ |
| Fun | ✪✪ |

# 6.53 **Putting it into practice**

---

**Preparation** None
**Applicability** Those setting up to sell coaching
**Time taken** A day
**Where/when** Before you set yourself up

---

If you are setting yourself up as a coach and wish to attract clients, you need to think through how you are going to go about this. Think carefully about the area in which you are coaching and who your target customers are. How will they get to know of you? Once they do, how will you convince them that you can add value? How will you continue to generate business while working with existing clients?

These are all questions that face a small business or sole trader and once you are in the marketplace you will be no different. Your business plan is the first area to consider. Think about how you will earn money. How much will people be willing to pay? The key factor is what is the competition charging? There are subtleties to consider here. Is there any competition? Are they offering exactly what you will? Is their area exactly the same as yours? Is their experience the same as yours? You will need to reflect the answers to these questions in your price. Now, how many customers are you likely to have and what will you earn as a result of working with them? You might want to plan on two levels – one optimistic and one pessimistic. Then think about your initial expenditure and any ongoing costs. What marketing will you do and what will it cost? Will you be renting or hiring a venue? What other costs will you incur? Having thought these through, you can do a rough financial projection. Don't worry too much about profit. Focus more on cash. Start with the cash that you put into the business to get it going and then month by month project what you will spend and what you will earn. This sort of cash flow is critical to you. Thinking through when you get paid (do you offer any payment terms or do you get cash on the nail?), and when you have to pay (which bills get paid as they are incurred and which ones have delays in payment – are there any paid in advance?), and this will allow you to plan the cash more accurately.

Finally, focus on the detail of the marketing. Will you have a business card and what will it look like? Will you put out flyers or posters? Where? What will they say? Once people do come to you, what system will you use to keep track of them, their targets and their progress? Answer all of these questions and you are well on the way to having a plan that will even keep your bank manager happy.

| | |
|---|---|
| Personal coaching | ✪✪✪✪ |
| Team coaching | ✪✪✪✪ |
| Applicability to business | ✪ |
| Development of you | ✪✪✪ |
| Fun | ✪✪ |

# 6.54 | *Quick results*

**Preparation** None
**Applicability** Where the coachee needs results quickly
**Time taken** An hour or two with the coachee
**Where/when** As soon as you can

You will meet a coachee who accepts everything that the two of you talk through about their needs and the time that it will take to make these happen, but who still wants results now. There are often things that you can do to offer quick results. There are also, more importantly, things that you can do to focus a coachee into a more realistic time frame.

If you are OK about rushing their development and looking for quick results, then you jointly need to look at their time. In general, the way to move faster in most fields that you will coach in is to spend a greater proportion of your time on developing the skill in the coachee. If the coachee is willing and able to do this you could plan accordingly. Another important factor to consider here is that this plan is likely to commit a greater proportion of your time because the targets will be coming around sooner.

If you feel that rushing their development is not appropriate, then you need to work with them on the reasons why they need the results now. It might be that they have set themselves a particular deadline and cannot move to change it. Why is the deadline important? How much is the attachment to it real and how much is in their heads? Exploring the pressure they are putting on themselves could help to relieve it.

Do not push too hard one way or the other – to accept the deadline or to refuse it. Remember that they are the people you are helping, not you. Remember that these are their goals, not yours. Explore them, develop them and be honest with them if you feel that they are unrealistic, but ultimately this is their life.

| | |
|---|---|
| Personal coaching | ✪✪✪✪ |
| Team coaching | ✪✪ |
| Applicability to business | ✪✪✪ |
| Development of you | ✪ |
| Fun | ✪✪ |

# 6.55 | *Reluctance to improve*

---

**Preparation** Exercise 6.49, *Positive affirmations*
**Applicability** Any coachee who holds back on improvement
**Time taken** An hour or two
**Where/when** Any time and anywhere

---

At the other end of the spectrum from those wanting results immediately are those who seem determined not to improve themselves. At times, it seems almost as though they are happy to be where they are, no matter how much they insist that they are ready for change.

The first and most important thing to say is that this state may seem like wilful ignorance but it rarely is. It is most often the case that people who seem reluctant to improve are actually those who cannot believe in this improvement in themselves. They would happily move to a new them. They would happily improve themselves, but they know deep inside themselves that they are where they are meant to be and that they are unable to get any better. They are wrong. Part of your role as coach is to show them that they are wrong and to help them to lift themselves above the low self-esteem that has caused them to be stuck.

A useful short exercise to use in this situation is to hunt down what it is that is causing them to limit themselves. Look at exercise 6.49, *Positive affirmations*. You will need to be able to take the coachee through this after doing this exercise here.

Get the coachee to think back through their life and to recall, as clearly as they can, any occasion when they have been told that they are not good or not able. This may even have been given as praise but turned into a limit. For instance, 'You're so bright you'll always be top of the class' becomes a limiting statement as soon as you're not at the top. Now ask them to write a list of these statements. Then get them to choose one that they believe has affected them and to write a letter (with no intention of ever sending it) to the person that made the comment.

Finally, get them to create some positive affirmations that counter the limits that they feel.

| | |
|---|---|
| Personal coaching | ✪✪✪✪ |
| Team coaching | ✪✪ |
| Applicability to business | ✪✪✪✪ |
| Development of you | ✪✪✪ |
| Fun | ✪✪✪ |

# 6.56 | *Role models*

**Preparation** None
**Applicability** All coaching situations
**Time taken** Half an hour to an hour
**Where/when** With the coachee as part of a regular coaching session

A key tool that you have as a coach is to help the coachee to find role models who will assist them in forming some of the skills that they need to improve. The role models that they use need not be people that they know or that they can interact with, but they do need to be observable. That is, the coachee must be able to see and analyse their performance so as to learn from it.

Where the discipline that you are coaching is in the public domain, such as sports, theatre, or any public performance, then observation of the performance is easy. More than this, finding role models is easy. Where the discipline that you are coaching is more private, such as most business, then you are relying more on your network. In this instance, you will either need to get the coachee together with the role model in some way or pass on observations to them. The coachee themself may know of someone who they admire and who is ahead of them in performance. If this is the case, then they should use them as a role model and you will need to find ways of observing their performance so as to challenge and draw out the coachee.

Books can be a useful source of business role models. Since the 1980s, there has been an increase in business autobiographies, biographies and case studies. They provide useful insights into the performance of others. They should also be taken with a pinch of salt. Whoever wrote them, there is likely to be an angle. There is likely to be a bias in the perspective in one way or another. Still, they are useful for all that.

Sit down with your coachee and discuss the area of role models. Check with them whether they have any that they could suggest. In turn, you can suggest any ideas that you have. If you happen to find a role model that appeals to the coachee and works for you, then you need to discuss ways that the coachee can get closer to them, find out more about them and generally learn from them.

| | |
|---|---|
| Personal coaching | ✪✪✪✪ |
| Team coaching | ✪✪✪ |
| Applicability to business | ✪✪✪✪ |
| Development of you | ✪✪ |
| Fun | ✪✪✪ |

## 6.57 | *Sharing what you know*

**Preparation** None
**Applicability** Where you have knowledge in the discipline being coached
**Time taken** An hour or so to plan
**Where/when** Early in the coaching relationship

So far, I have gone to great lengths to stress that coaching is not about you imparting your knowledge to the coachee, it is about you drawing knowledge from the coachee. Still, there will be times when you know something that would be useful to the coachee and would help with their development. It would be absurd for you to withhold this in support of a pure model of coaching. The reason I have stressed this so strongly is that most people's bias would be towards telling what they know rather than extracting from the coachee. Overcoming this bias has meant erring on the other side of the equation.

When you do have knowledge that would be potentially useful to the coachee, you need to think about how and when it is best imparted. This will rarely be at the start of the coaching relationship. It is important that initial progress is made on the basis of what they know already. Your knowledge will wait. So, plan within the coaching relationship time for imparting this knowledge.

The next consideration is how is the knowledge best imparted? To what degree is your knowledge available in books? If there are some good books around the area of knowledge that you are working on, then guiding your coachee through these could be a good way of developing them without needing to be their teacher. What about courses, classes or other forms of tuition; are there any you could recommend? You could also, perhaps, recommend others who could teach your coachee. Finally, as a last resort, there's you. You acting as teacher.

OK, I've done it again. I have stressed the need for you to stay away from the teaching and stick to the coaching. I apologize. As I said earlier, some teaching may be entirely appropriate, but think hard before you start.

| | |
|---|---|
| Personal coaching | ✪✪✪✪ |
| Team coaching | ✪✪✪✪ |
| Applicability to business | ✪✪✪✪ |
| Development of you | ✪ |
| Fun | ✪✪✪ |

# 6.58 | *Slow progress*

---

**Preparation** Exercise 6.55, *Reluctance to improve*
**Applicability** Whenever progress is slower than planned
**Time taken** An hour or two
**Where/when** With the coachee in private

---

We discussed earlier, in 6.55, *Reluctance to improve*, the coachee who has limiting beliefs that slow down their improvement. There are other possible ways that progress can be slowed. This exercise is about identifying the cause of slow progress as a first step to resolving it. These questions are best explored with the coachee, although there are some that you could answer alone if need be.

The first thing to consider is that you and the coachee might have been too optimistic in the initial goal setting. Looking back at the progress you expected, does it still feel reasonable? If you coach others in this same discipline, would you expect the same of them? If you have any doubts about this, start the goal-setting process again and develop a new set of goals as though you were at the start of the process.

Next, are there external factors inhibiting progress? Does your coachee have the ability to practise or develop in the way they need when they are not with you? Do they have the resources they need?

Now both of you need to look at the coachee. Are they as committed to these goals as they were when they started? Are they working as hard as they said they would at the start? Are they able to make available the time that they need?

Finally, you need to look at the coaching relationship. Are you working together well? Are there areas where you are getting in the way of their progress? This may be the hardest area of all to explore, because the relationship you will have developed with the coachee will probably have made it OK to explore their performance, but less OK to explore yours.

Once you have been through each of these areas you need to write down the results and decide what needs to change. This may be the targets or it may be part of the way you are working towards the targets. Whatever changes you decide to make, you need to re-establish the plan that you have, revise any targets, change any work plan and develop new approaches. You might also have to make commitments about your end of the deal.

| | |
|---|---|
| Personal coaching | ✪✪✪✪ |
| Team coaching | ✪✪✪✪ |
| Applicability to business | ✪✪✪✪ |
| Development of you | ✪✪✪ |
| Fun | ✪✪ |

## 6.59 | *Stop and think*

**Preparation** None
**Applicability** Coaching and beyond
**Time taken** An hour or two
**Where/when** Every couple of months

This exercise is not specific to coaching. It applies to anything in life where we get onto a treadmill that carries us forward with its own momentum. If your coaching relationship is lasting for any length of time it is likely that aspects of it will become like this, even if it doesn't seem that way to you right now.

In your own personal plan, build in a personal review with yourself every couple of months. This review is to look at what you are doing, how you are doing it and to think through whether it is still giving you the buzz you would like it to.

Sit down alone with a pad of paper, a pen, a cup of tea or coffee and plenty of time. Now list for yourself all of the things you are currently doing that you love. This list is not related solely to work, all of your life should be included. Now write down all of the things that you do that feel like chores. The things that you feel you have to do. Now, with the first list take each of the statements and write, 'I choose to <whatever the statement is> because…'. Write here why you choose to do this and list as many because statements as you can. Now with the second list take each of the statements and write, 'I have to <whatever the statement is> or else…'. Write here what will happen if you don't do this. Write as many or else statements as you can.

Go through each of these statements and, as objectively as you are able, write next to each the letter T, the letter F or a question mark. T if the statement is absolutely true. F is the statement is false or true only in part. Question mark if you don't know. Now for all F statements rewrite a statement that is objectively true.

The reason for this writing is to give you ammunition to think through your life and to address anything in it that you would like to change. Use some of the change tools such as 6.49, *Positive affirmations*, and 6.50, *Positive visualization*, to work on these.

| | |
|---|---|
| Personal coaching | ✪ |
| Team coaching | ✪ |
| Applicability to business | ✪ |
| Development of you | ✪✪✪✪ |
| Fun | ✪✪ |

# 6.60 | **Strategy**

---

**Preparation** None
**Applicability** All coaching situations
**Time taken** A few hours
**Where/when** With the coachee before you commence coaching

---

When coaching someone else, or even when working on yourself, it is useful to have a notion of how to think through a strategy. The difficulty with summarizing this is that in one sense strategy can mean anything you want it to mean. It will also mean different things from one coaching situation to another.

The first thing to think about when putting together a strategy is the timescale you are working to. If you have five years to work with your coachee, your view of strategy will be very different to having a couple of months. Knowing the timescale, it is useful to divide it into shorter chunks of time for your thinking. I find that between 5 and 10 chunks is a useful guideline. The period closest to you should have chunks that are small and the further away you go the chunks should get longer. For instance, if thinking on a five-year time frame you might decide to have the last couple of years as one chunk, years two and three as two other chunks, the last six months of year one as another chunk and then monthly chunks for the first six months. This gives you the ability to think about targets in a focused way.

An important point about strategy is that it works best in reverse. Thinking about where you want to end up and then working backwards – to achieve this in the last period I need to achieve this in the one before – and so on. I'm not sure why this is. I have tried working both ways in my thinking and have found that working forwards from where you are now produces incremental thinking, while working backwards allows leaps of imagination and faith.

What you decide to write down to summarize your strategy is up to you and the coachee. I would strongly recommend getting something down on paper. Remember that this is going to be the basis of your thinking until you decide to replace it. I tend to write some background – what this is for, who it pertains to, why we're bothering, etc. I then tend to describe the end goal and the reasons why it is important. Finally, I lay out the time periods and specify what will be achieved in each and how we intend to make that happen. Having done all of this, remember that you can change your minds (both you and the coachee). This document is a guide, not a millstone.

| | |
|---|---|
| Personal coaching | ✪✪✪✪ |
| Team coaching | ✪✪✪✪ |
| Applicability to business | ✪✪✪✪ |
| Development of you | ✪✪✪ |
| Fun | ✪✪ |

## 6.61 | *Teaching versus coaching*

---

**Preparation** None
**Applicability** All coaches
**Time taken** Very little
**Where/when** Any time

---

I have a confession to make. Sometimes I teach. Indeed, I'm doing it now. This book is a teaching vehicle and not a coaching vehicle. The bottom line is that there are times when teaching is actually a necessary part of coaching. I have said earlier that it should be a last resort. I stress again that the reason for saying this is that most of us fall more naturally into a teaching role than a coaching role. We feel that if we are asked to develop someone's expertise, then the way to do this is to show our own prowess first. The example of Doug Blevins, the Miami Dolphins' kicking coach, should dispel the illusion that you need to be good at it to be able to coach it. Doug teaches the Dolphins' players to kick field goals. He is apparently an outstanding coach. The remarkable thing is that Doug has not only never kicked a field goal, he has never walked in his life. He is wheelchair-bound. It is his coaching skill and his ability to extract the essence of every tiny movement that the players make that causes him to excel. It is not his ability to kick a ball.

My bet is, though, that there are times when Doug will teach aspects of the craft to his players. He may well work with them on analysing what they do, on setting performance targets and on working obsessively towards those targets. He will also, at times, point out that a foot at this angle will perform better than a foot at that angle. There will be things that he knows that the players need to know. The essence of coaching is that these will be the exceptions, not the rule. He will coach mostly and teach rarely.

Take a little time to think about some recent coaching encounters and estimate what percentage of your time you were teaching and what percentage you were coaching. Anything more than a few per cent in the first category is likely to be too much.

| | |
|---|---|
| Personal coaching | ✪✪✪✪ |
| Team coaching | ✪✪✪✪ |
| Applicability to business | ✪✪✪✪ |
| Development of you | ✪✪✪✪ |
| Fun | ✪ |

# 6.62 | *Team coaching*

---

**Preparation** None
**Applicability** Any team coaching
**Time taken** Very little
**Where/when** Any time

---

In 6.34, *Individual coaching*, I tried to lay out some of my ideas on coaching an individual. This is the other end of the spectrum where you are coaching a team. Almost all of the exercises in this book are applicable to team coaching and so there's not a great deal of need for this section. However, there are a couple of points that need to be covered.

First, there's playing favourites. You need to be obsessively careful that you are not seen to favour one member of the team over others. We can all remember awful sports coaches (normally sports teachers at school), who focused their effort and their praise on their star players and left the rest of the team to look after themselves. Doing this forgets that it is the team that performs, not just individuals. If these coaches really thought through what they were doing, they would realize that they should either learn to coach the whole team or dispense with all but their stars and play with only a few players on the field. This latter option is an obvious nonsense, but it is the ultimate implication of playing favourites in this way. You need to have a strong relationship with every member of the team, not just a few.

Next, there's the distribution of effort between developing the team and developing the individuals. Having said that the team performs not just as individuals, but it is clear that the team is made up of those individuals. Increasing their level of skill increases the team's level of skill. However, the team is more than the sum of its parts. A team that works well achieves more than that number of individuals possibly could. At least half of your time should be working with individuals within the team and the other half on developing the overall level of team performance.

Finally, there's the winning attitude. Developing a team that outperforms any possible targets comes about as a result of convincing them of their own invincibility. Together they can work miracles. They only need to be given the chance.

If you coach a team, score yourself against the three areas above. How do they pan out in your case?

| | |
|---|---|
| Personal coaching | ✪ |
| Team coaching | ✪✪✪✪ |
| Applicability to business | ✪✪✪✪ |
| Development of you | ✪✪ |
| Fun | ✪✪ |

## 6.63 | *The future is a foreign country*

**Preparation** None
**Applicability** All coaches
**Time taken** One or two days
**Where/when** Whenever

Again, we're looking at the nature of time. As I have said before, the only point in time that you can make a difference to is now. You cannot affect the past and you can only plan for the future. The real issue here is one of balance. Being too future focused creates worry. Yet you have to have a focus on the future so as to create and follow plans. You need to ensure two things. First, that the majority of your focus is now and, second, that your focus and your coachee's focus align. A mismatch of your view of time can cause confusion.

To address the first of these, here is an exercise that can be difficult to follow because it requires you to concentrate on your thinking processes at the same time as living your life. The results can be interesting. For the next day, or two if you can manage, notice where your thoughts are. Are you thinking about what is happening now? Are you thinking about what is about to happen? Are you thinking about what has happened? Carry a notebook around with you and every hour or so note down where your thinking time has gone.

The very act of doing this exercise will affect the outcome because being aware of your thinking will change your thinking. Don't worry about that, this is not science and there is no precision in it. At the end of the day or two days, add up the proportions of time in your notebook and look at the total. Also, look at the individual hour totals. If you are anything like me you'll find that when you are really busy you are very *now* focused. When you are under pressure you become very *future* focused and when you are idling or feeling maudlin you become very *past* focused.

| | |
|---|---|
| Personal coaching | ✪ |
| Team coaching | ✪ |
| Applicability to business | ✪ |
| Development of you | ✪✪✪✪ |
| Fun | ✪✪✪ |

# 6.64 | *The past is a foreign country*

**Preparation** Do exercise 6.63, *The future is a foreign country*
**Applicability** All coaching relationships
**Time taken** A few minutes plus some time for discussion
**Where/when** Wherever you and your coachee can meet

One final look at the nature of time. To repeat myself, the only point in time that you can make a difference to is now. The past cannot be affected and the future is only in plans. Being stuck in the past creates inertia and an inability to move forward – yet you have to focus on the past in order to learn lessons. Yet again, it is a question of balance. I said in the last exercise that you need to ensure two things. First, that the majority of your focus is now and, second, that your focus and your coachee's focus align. Do exercise 6.63, *The future is a foreign country*, which addresses the first of these and then this exercise, which addresses the second.

You and your coachee should both have a sheet of paper and then draw three circles that represent past, present and future. You should not be able to see each other's sheets. The circles can be any size; the relative size expresses the relative importance of each of these periods of time in your mind. They can be anywhere on the paper; the relative position indicates the relationship between each of these periods of time. They can be in any order or any position.

Once you have done this, compare the results. What similarities are there in the relative size, position and relationship of the circles? What differences are there? Do these similarities and differences tell you anything about your relative notions of time? Does what they tell you give you any insights into your relationship? There are no right and wrong answers to this. Whatever you come up with is right for you. Similarly, there is no notion of you trying to change your coachee's view of time or vice versa. This exercise is about understanding, not convergence.

| | |
|---|---|
| Personal coaching | ✪✪✪✪ |
| Team coaching | ✪✪✪ |
| Applicability to business | ✪✪✪✪ |
| Development of you | ✪✪✪✪ |
| Fun | ✪✪✪ |

# 6.65 | *The reluctant coach*

**Preparation** None
**Applicability** Anyone who doesn't want to be a coach
**Time taken** A couple of hours
**Where/when** Now

I have assumed throughout this book that you have eagerly volunteered for the role of coach and that this is something that is important to you. What if you have found yourself forced into the role and you are reading this book in an attempt to find out what you've let yourself in for? Well, my first piece of advice is, don't do it! That's not to say that you shouldn't be a coach. It's something that I love doing and that spills over into many non-coaching relationships. What I'm saying is that you should start coaching only when you know what you're letting yourself in for and only when you're happy that this is something you want.

OK, having said that there will always be situations where you feel you have no choice (or rather that the alternative choices you can see are unpalatable). You might have a boss who has decided that you will be a coach and who's view of the world does not allow for argument. If this is the case, my first question would be why are you staying there, but we'll leave that one for now.

If you are determined to go ahead with this, then you need to get rid of the reluctance. As with anything, coaching is something that works best if you do it with joy, energy and love. Be a coach. Be a great coach. But do it willingly. How can you do this? Well, I guess it's predictable that I'd suggest that you coach yourself.

Do exercise 6.50, *Positive visualization*, creating a visualization for yourself of a great day coaching. A day where you are working as the best, the most skilful, the most able coach in the world. Additionally, you could try a symbolic visualization where you create symbols for the reluctance you feel and create a visualization that destroys them.

Finally, write some affirmations (6.49, *Positive affirmations*) that create you as a world-class coach. Listen for the voice in your head that argues against you and write affirmations to negate this voice. Once you've done this, leap in!

| | |
|---|---|
| Personal coaching | ✪ |
| Team coaching | ✪ |
| Applicability to business | ✪ |
| Development of you | ✪✪✪✪ |
| Fun | ✪✪✪ |

# 6.66 | *Using the ADAPT model*

---

**Preparation** Read Chapter 4 – A coaching model
**Applicability** All coaches
**Time taken half** An hour to check through
**Where/when** Any time

---

First a reminder of the ADAPT model (see Chapter 4, A Coaching Model). ADAPT stands for:

A – Assess current performance
D – Develop a plan
A – Act on the plan
P – Progress check
T – Tell and ask

The questions that spring to mind with a model like this are: when do you use it, when do you do without it, when do you deviate from it? As always, there are no blanket answers. I find that models like this are similar to training wheels on a bike. When you're starting out they are a necessary reassurance, but as you get better they start to become an encumbrance, and once your skill has reached the level where you can balance without them, then you're far better off getting rid of them than keeping them.

When you are using the model, remember that it is just that – a model. It is not reality and doesn't claim to be reality. If the real world indicates that you behave in one way and the model indicates that you behave in another, go with the real world every time. Having said that, the model is general enough that it is unlikely to get in the way, it's just that your interpretation of it will change from situation to situation.

At the point where you do without the model, it will be because you are able to manage intuitively to do the things that the model includes without forcing them into a structure. If you are in this situation, then go through a recent coaching session (or series of sessions), and assess where they were in the model. What did they cover, what did they miss out? I find this a useful check every so often just to ensure that I am covering all of the ground and covering it in the right order.

| Personal coaching | ✪✪✪ |
| Team coaching | ✪✪✪ |
| Applicability to business | ✪✪✪ |
| Development of you | ✪✪✪✪ |
| Fun | ✪✪ |

# 6.67 | *Vision*

---

**Preparation** None
**Applicability** Any team coaching where a vision would act as a focus
**Time taken** An hour to a day
**Where/when** Whenever you can get the team together

---

Many companies have vision statements. In general, they are utterly useless. They are useless, primarily, because nobody can remember them and, secondarily, because they are written as corporate blah blah rather than as meaningful or emotional statements. Over the years, I have developed a view that visions are useful. They are useful if, and only if, everyone affected by them is committed to them and is able to remember them. Partly in support of the first of these, and largely in support of the second, I reckon that visions should be a single word; at most a very short phrase. If you feel your team would benefit from having a vision as a focus, then get them together and go through this short exercise.

Collect together any words that they can think of that describe the team – ideally on a flipchart. These could be positives or negatives. Now get words that describe where the team wants to be. Then move away from the team and get them to talk, one by one, about things that they can be passionate about, their families, their friends, movies, their hobbies – anything that arouses passion. As they talk, capture words. Now get everyone to peruse all of the flipcharts that you've covered (and there should be quite a few), and circle three words (each) that they feel embody the vision of the team. Some words will be circled once, some many times. Now facilitate a discussion where they whittle down this list to a final word or very short phrase. How do you collectively feel about this as a vision? If it works, then you will be able to relate it to every single activity that the team undertakes and improve that activity with reference to it.

Personal coaching     ✪
Team coaching     ✪✪✪✪
Applicability to business     ✪✪✪✪
Development of you     ✪✪
Fun     ✪✪✪

# 6.68 | **When to coach**

---

**Preparation** None
**Applicability** Managers who wish to coach
**Time taken** An hour
**Where/when** Any time alone

---

For some, the question of when to coach is nonsensical. If you are a full-time professional coach, then you coach when you go to work. You will probably find yourself coaching at other times, too. This question is actually directed at those who have another role, such as manager, and want to add coaching to their repertoire of skills. When does your normal job extend into a coaching role? The simple answer is any time you choose.

Coaching is a skill that enhances most supervisory relationships because it changes them from being boss/subordinate to a more equal footing. You might feel that this is inappropriate for your management style, for your organization or for your staff. It might be, but it probably isn't. Most people in most organizations with most staff can coach effectively in most supervisory relationships. If you genuinely feel that you can't, then you're either wrong or else yours is not one of the 'most' situations I've just been talking about.

To take a look at this, sit down with a pen and paper and map out your last week in as much detail as you can. What meetings did you have (formal and informal)? What work did you do on your own? What interactions did you have with your boss, peers, staff and colleagues? Once you have done this, mark beside each one in a different colour a letter to indicate whether you could have used coaching skills in that interaction. I would suggest Y for yes and N for no. Now analyse your sheet of paper and look for the common threads. Where could coaching have worked and where could it not?

Be prepared to challenge yourself in this. If you took my stance that most interactions could benefit from a coaching relationship and you have a number of Ns, then ask yourself how could you make it work (whether you ultimately choose to or not). Whatever your results from this, just the process of paying attention to the possibility will extend your potential use of coaching.

| | |
|---|---|
| Personal coaching | ✪✪✪ |
| Team coaching | ✪✪✪ |
| Applicability to business | ✪✪✪✪ |
| Development of you | ✪✪✪✪ |
| Fun | ✪✪ |

# 6.69 | *Wu wei*

---

**Preparation** None
**Applicability** Everyone
**Time taken** A lifetime
**Where/when** Now and from now

---

This is not an exercise so much as a philosophy of life. Wu wei is a Chinese expression that means doing by not doing or doing with least effort. It is the principal behind Tai Chi and many other martial arts. It is a philosophy that leads to a greater efficiency of life and a more relaxed style.

In the context of this book, I am obviously applying it to coaching. My point is that coaching is something best done with least effort. You may put in a great deal of work with and for a coachee but never make it look hard. Indeed, it is best if it isn't hard. Make it your business to display in your coaching style an effortless grace that acts as a role model to your coachee(s). Make it a point also to ensure that you meet all of the commitments you make and to act as a role model in terms of the work that you do and your professionalism. Having a coach who doesn't meet commitments is no role model for a coachee.

If you want to finish with an exercise that will help you to develop this philosophy, call your local sports centre or community centre and find out where you can study Tai Chi. It may be a long-term commitment, but then that's what this book has been about, isn't it?

| | |
|---|---|
| Personal coaching | ✪✪✪✪ |
| Team coaching | ✪✪✪✪ |
| Applicability to business | ✪✪✪✪ |
| Development of you | ✪✪✪✪ |
| Fun | ✪✪✪✪ |

# 7

# OTHER SOURCES

# THERE'S MORE

Instant Coaching *is merely a taster to get you started on the coaching road or to give you a boost along it if already started. This short chapter is a resource kit for going beyond* Instant Coaching.

## THEORY

In putting together the *Instant* series of books, the focus has been on the practical rather than on the theory underlying the exercises. If you would like to explore more of the theory, check the Creativity Unleashed online bookshop at **http://www.cul.co.uk/books**, which provides plenty of information and direct buying links to the biggest online bookshops in the UK and the US. It's also worth checking there for more up-to-date references, and for books that are hard to get hold of in the UK.

## BOOKS

*Coaching Books*
Miles Downey, *Effective Coaching*, Orion Business, 1999
A general and fairly broad book on coaching.

Ian Fleming and Allan J D Taylor, *The Coaching Pocketbook*, Management Pocketbooks, 1998
A very small book that does a great job of outlining what coaching is about and making lots of use of keywords and cartoons.

Bill Foster and Karen R Seeker, *Coaching for Peak Performance*, Kogan Page, 1998
A book in the management skills series that is again aimed at the workplace, primarily at managers and supervisors.

Eileen Mulligan, *Life Coaching*, Judy Piaktus, 1999
A book with the subtitle 'Change your life in 7 days'. Lively and readable.

Max Landsberg, *The Tao of Coaching*, HarperCollins, 1997
A book primarily aimed at the work situation.

Jinny S Ditzler, *Your Best Year Yet!*, Thorson, 1994
A useful book that has affected my life and also given me some tools to use in coaching others.

*Other books for subjects mentioned in the text*
Paul Birch and Brian Clegg, *Instant Creativity*, Kogan Page, 1999

Julia Cameron, *The Artist's Way*, Macmillan, 1995

Shakti Gawain, *Creative Visualisation*, Nataraj Publishing, 1995

## Online Coaching

As always, the Internet can be a useful source of information on this subject. The one caveat is that any links that are suggested in a book will quickly become out of date. Using your favourite search engine will allow you to find links of your own, but you will need to make your search specific so as not to be overwhelmed by responses. If you do not use search engines regularly, you might want to try Altavista **www.altavista.com** or Yahoo **www.yahoo.com**

A couple of references that might stay current are listed below.

**http://www.ncf.org.uk**
Coaching from a sporting perspective.

**http://www.nlp-community.com/jancoaching.htm**
An interesting article on coaching from a neuro-linguistic programming perspective.

# APPENDIX:
# THE SELECTOR

This appendix contains a set of tables that will help you to find the activity that best suits your needs. The first set of tables is sorted by the star ratings for each activity so as to make it easy to pick out an appropriate activity. Next come tables sorted by preparation time and time taken.

# ACTIVITIES IN PERSONAL COACHING ORDER

This table sorts the activities by the personal coaching star rating. Those at the top have the highest star rating, those at the bottom the lowest.

| Ref | Title | Ref | Title |
|-----|-------|-----|-------|
| ✪✪✪✪ | | 6.43 | Measuring improvement |
| 6.1 | Aiming high enough | 6.45 | Now is all you can do |
| 6.3 | Backing off | 6.46 | 'Now look what you've done' |
| 6.4 | Being realistic | 6.47 | Overcoming a lifetime of learning |
| 6.5 | Being unrealistic | 6.48 | Planning to coach |
| 6.6 | Building relationships | 6.51 | Problems, problems, problems |
| 6.7 | Catch them doing it right | 6.53 | Putting it into practice |
| 6.8 | Checking for understanding | 6.54 | Quick results |
| 6.13 | Coaching your boss | 6.55 | Reluctance to improve |
| 6.15 | Coaching yourself | 6.56 | Role models |
| 6.16 | Delegation | 6.57 | Sharing what you know |
| 6.17 | Developing the right environment | 6.58 | Slow progress |
| 6.18 | Developing trust | 6.60 | Strategy |
| 6.20 | Eliminate the negative | 6.61 | Teaching versus coaching |
| 6.21 | Emergencies | 6.64 | The past is a foreign country |
| 6.22 | Engendering belief | 6.69 | Wu wei |
| 6.23 | Establishing pace | ✪✪✪ | |
| 6.24 | Establishing the two-way process | 6.2 | Appraisals |
| 6.25 | Following up | 6.31 | Going the extra mile |
| 6.26 | From why to how | 6.49 | Positive affirmations |
| 6.27 | Getting beneath anxiety | 6.50 | Positive visualization |
| 6.28 | Giving feedback | 6.52 | Pushing and yielding |
| 6.29 | Goal setting | 6.66 | Using the ADAPT model |
| 6.30 | Goals | 6.68 | When to coach |
| 6.32 | 'I can't do it' | ✪ | |
| 6.33 | 'If only they wouldn't…' | 6.9 | Checking your coachfulness |
| 6.34 | Individual coaching | 6.10 | Coaching as an organizational |
| 6.35 | Killing fear | | norm |
| 6.36 | Knowing what you know | 6.11 | Coaching outside work |
| 6.37 | Learning and learning styles | 6.12 | Coaching with others |
| 6.38 | Learning to believe | 6.14 | Coaching your peers |
| 6.39 | Lecturing and hectoring | 6.19 | Doing yourself out of a job |
| 6.40 | Letting go of the solution | 6.41 | Love |
| 6.42 | Marking time | 6.44 | Mission |

# ACTIVITIES IN TEAM COACHING ORDER

This table sorts the activities by the team coaching star rating. Those at the top have the highest star rating, those at the bottom the lowest.

| 6.49 | Positive affirmations | 6.63 | The future is a foreign country |
| 6.59 | Stop and think | 6.65 | The reluctant coach |

# ACTIVITIES IN APPLICABILITY TO BUSINESS ORDER

This table sorts the activities by the applicability to business star rating. Those at the top have the highest star rating, those at the bottom the lowest.

| Ref | Title | Ref | Title |
|-----|-------|-----|-------|
| ✪✪✪✪ | | 6.39 | Lecturing and hectoring |
| 6.1 | Aiming high enough | 6.40 | Letting go of the solution |
| 6.2 | Appraisals | 6.42 | Marking time |
| 6.3 | Backing off | 6.43 | Measuring improvement |
| 6.4 | Being realistic | 6.44 | Mission |
| 6.5 | Being unrealistic | 6.45 | Now is all you can do |
| 6.6 | Building relationships | 6.46 | 'Now look what you've done' |
| 6.7 | Catch them doing it right | 6.47 | Overcoming a lifetime of learning |
| 6.8 | Checking for understanding | 6.51 | Problems, problems, problems |
| 6.9 | Checking your coachfulness | 6.55 | Reluctance to improve |
| 6.10 | Coaching as an organizational | 6.56 | Role models |
| | norm | 6.57 | Sharing what you know |
| 6.12 | Coaching with others | 6.58 | Slow progress |
| 6.13 | Coaching your boss | 6.60 | Strategy |
| 6.14 | Coaching your peers | 6.61 | Teaching versus coaching |
| 6.16 | Delegation | 6.62 | Team coaching |
| 6.17 | Developing the right environment | 6.64 | The past is a foreign country |
| 6.19 | Doing yourself out of a job | 6.67 | Vision |
| 6.21 | Emergencies | 6.68 | When to coach |
| 6.22 | Engendering belief | 6.69 | Wu wei |
| 6.23 | Establishing pace | ✪✪✪ | |
| 6.24 | Establishing the two-way process | 6.18 | Developing trust |
| 6.25 | Following up | 6.20 | Eliminate the negative |
| 6.26 | From why to how | 6.31 | Going the extra mile |
| 6.27 | Getting beneath anxiety | 6.52 | Pushing and yielding |
| 6.28 | Giving feedback | 6.54 | Quick results |
| 6.29 | Goal setting | 6.66 | Using the ADAPT model |
| 6.30 | Goals | ✪✪ | |
| 6.32 | 'I can't do it' | 6.15 | Coaching yourself |
| 6.33 | 'If only they wouldn't…' | 6.48 | Planning to coach |
| 6.34 | Individual coaching | 6.49 | Positive affirmations |
| 6.35 | Killing fear | 6.50 | Positive visualization |
| 6.36 | Knowing what you know | ✪ | |
| 6.37 | Learning and learning styles | 6.11 | Coaching outside work |
| 6.38 | Learning to believe | 6.41 | Love |

| 6.53 | Putting it into practice | 6.63 | The future is a foreign country |
|------|--------------------------|------|--------------------------------|
| 6.59 | Stop and think | 6.65 | The reluctant coach |

# ACTIVITIES IN DEVELOPMENT OF YOU ORDER

This table sorts the activities by the development of you star rating. Those at the top have the highest star rating, those at the bottom the lowest.

| Ref | Title | Ref | Title |
|-----|-------|-----|-------|
| ✪✪✪✪ | | 6.33 | 'If only they wouldn't…' |
| 6.7 | Catch them doing it right | 6.34 | Individual coaching |
| 6.9 | Checking your coachfulness | 6.35 | Killing fear |
| 6.11 | Coaching outside work | 6.36 | Knowing what you know |
| 6.15 | Coaching yourself | 6.53 | Putting it into practice |
| 6.18 | Developing trust | 6.55 | Reluctance to improve |
| 6.19 | Doing yourself out of a job | 6.58 | Slow progress |
| 6.31 | Going the extra mile | 6.60 | Strategy |
| 6.38 | Learning to believe | ✪✪ | |
| 6.39 | Lecturing and hectoring | 6.10 | Coaching as an organizational |
| 6.41 | Love | | norm |
| 6.48 | Planning to coach | 6.28 | Giving feedback |
| 6.49 | Positive affirmations | 6.29 | Goal setting |
| 6.50 | Positive visualization | 6.40 | Letting go of the solution |
| 6.52 | Pushing and yielding | 6.43 | Measuring improvement |
| 6.59 | Stop and think | 6.44 | Mission |
| 6.61 | Teaching versus coaching | 6.45 | Now is all you can do |
| 6.63 | The future is a foreign country | 6.46 | 'Now look what you've done' |
| 6.64 | The past is a foreign country | 6.47 | Overcoming a lifetime of learning |
| 6.65 | The reluctant coach | 6.51 | Problems, problems, problems |
| 6.66 | Using the ADAPT model | 6.56 | Role models |
| 6.68 | When to coach | 6.62 | Team coaching |
| 6.69 | Wu wei | 6.67 | Vision |
| ✪✪✪ | | ✪ | |
| 6.3 | Backing off | 6.1 | Aiming high enough |
| 6.6 | Building relationships | 6.2 | Appraisals |
| 6.8 | Checking for understanding | 6.4 | Being realistic |
| 6.16 | Delegation | 6.5 | Being unrealistic |
| 6.17 | Developing the right environment | 6.12 | Coaching with others |
| 6.21 | Emergencies | 6.13 | Coaching your boss |
| 6.24 | Establishing the two-way process | 6.14 | Coaching your peers |
| 6.25 | Following up | 6.20 | Eliminate the negative |
| 6.26 | From why to how | 6.22 | Engendering belief |
| 6.27 | Getting beneath anxiety | 6.23 | Establishing pace |
| 6.30 | Goals | 6.32 | 'I can't do it' |

| 6.37 | Learning and learning styles | 6.54 | Quick results |
| 6.42 | Marking time | 6.57 | Sharing what you know |

# ACTIVITIES IN FUN ORDER

This table sorts the activities by the fun star rating. Those at the top have the highest star rating, those at the bottom the lowest.

| Ref | Title | Ref | Title |
|-----|-------|-----|-------|
| ✪✪✪✪ | | 6.27 | Getting beneath anxiety |
| 6.50 | Positive visualization | 6.28 | Giving feedback |
| 6.69 | Wu wei | 6.29 | Goal setting |
| ✪✪✪ | | 6.30 | Goals |
| 6.5 | Being unrealistic | 6.31 | Going the extra mile |
| 6.7 | Catch them doing it right | 6.33 | 'If only they wouldn't…' |
| 6.11 | Coaching outside work | 6.35 | Killing fear |
| 6.15 | Coaching yourself | 6.36 | Knowing what you know |
| 6.16 | Delegation | 6.37 | Learning and learning styles |
| 6.17 | Developing the right environment | 6.38 | Learning to believe |
| 6.19 | Doing yourself out of a job | 6.39 | Lecturing and hectoring |
| 6.21 | Emergencies | 6.40 | Letting go of the solution |
| 6.22 | Engendering belief | 6.42 | Marking time |
| 6.25 | Following up | 6.43 | Measuring improvement |
| 6.49 | Positive affirmations | 6.44 | Mission |
| 6.51 | Problems, problems, problems | 6.45 | Now is all you can do |
| 6.55 | Reluctance to improve | 6.46 | 'Now look what you've done' |
| 6.56 | Role models | 6.47 | Overcoming a lifetime of learning |
| 6.57 | Sharing what you know | 6.48 | Planning to coach |
| 6.63 | The future is a foreign country | 6.52 | Pushing and yielding |
| 6.64 | The past is a foreign country | 6.53 | Putting it into practice |
| 6.65 | The reluctant coach | 6.54 | Quick results |
| 6.67 | Vision | 6.58 | Slow progress |
| ✪✪ | | 6.59 | Stop and think |
| 6.6 | Building relationships | 6.60 | Strategy |
| 6.8 | Checking for understanding | 6.62 | Team coaching |
| 6.10 | Coaching as an organizational norm | 6.66 | Using the ADAPT model |
| 6.12 | Coaching with others | 6.68 | When to coach |
| 6.13 | Coaching your boss | ✪ | |
| 6.14 | Coaching your peers | 6.1 | Aiming high enough |
| 6.18 | Developing trust | 6.2 | Appraisals |
| 6.20 | Eliminate the negative | 6.3 | Backing off |
| 6.24 | Establishing the two-way process | 6.4 | Being realistic |
| 6.26 | From why to how | 6.9 | Checking your coachfulness |
| | | 6.23 | Establishing pace |

6.32   'I can't do it'            6.41   Love
6.34   Individual coaching       6.61   Teaching versus coaching

# ACTIVITIES IN ORDER OF EASE OF PREPARATION

This table sorts the activities by the ease with which you can prepare for them. Those at the top need no preparation and those at the bottom need a significant amount.

| Ref | Title | Ref | Title |
| --- | --- | --- | --- |
| 6.2 | Appraisals | 6.52 | Pushing and yielding |
| 6.3 | Backing off | 6.53 | Putting it into practice |
| 6.6 | Building relationships | 6.54 | Quick results |
| 6.7 | Catch them doing it right | 6.56 | Role models |
| 6.11 | Coaching outside work | 6.57 | Sharing what you know |
| 6.12 | Coaching with others | 6.59 | Stop and think |
| 6.13 | Coaching your boss | 6.60 | Strategy |
| 6.14 | Coaching your peers | 6.61 | Teaching versus coaching |
| 6.15 | Coaching yourself | 6.62 | Team coaching |
| 6.16 | Delegation | 6.63 | The future is a foreign country |
| 6.17 | Developing the right environment | 6.65 | The reluctant coach |
| 6.18 | Developing trust | 6.67 | Vision |
| 6.23 | Establishing pace | 6.68 | When to coach |
| 6.24 | Establishing the two-way process | 6.69 | Wu wei |
| 6.26 | From why to how | 6.9 | Checking your coachfulness |
| 6.27 | Getting beneath anxiety | 6.21 | Emergencies |
| 6.28 | Giving feedback | 6.25 | Following up |
| 6.31 | Going the extra mile | 6.29 | Goal setting |
| 6.32 | 'I can't do it' | 6.1 | Aiming high enough |
| 6.33 | 'If only they wouldn't…' | 6.4 | Being realistic |
| 6.35 | Killing fear | 6.5 | Being unrealistic |
| 6.36 | Knowing what you know | 6.8 | Checking for understanding |
| 6.37 | Learning and learning styles | 6.19 | Doing yourself out of a job |
| 6.38 | Learning to believe | 6.20 | Eliminate the negative |
| 6.39 | Lecturing and hectoring | 6.22 | Engendering belief |
| 6.40 | Letting go of the solution | 6.30 | Goals |
| 6.41 | Love | 6.34 | Individual coaching |
| 6.42 | Marking time | 6.46 | 'Now look what you've done' |
| 6.43 | Measuring improvement | 6.55 | Reluctance to improve |
| 6.44 | Mission | 6.58 | Slow progress |
| 6.45 | Now is all you can do | 6.64 | The past is a foreign country |
| 6.47 | Overcoming a lifetime of learning | 6.10 | Coaching as an organizational norm |
| 6.48 | Planning to coach | | |
| 6.49 | Positive affirmations | 6.51 | Problems, problems, problems |
| 6.50 | Positive visualization | 6.66 | Using the ADAPT model |

# ACTIVITIES IN ORDER OF TIME TAKEN

This table sorts the activities by the time that they take. Those at the top take least time and those at the bottom take significantly more.

| Ref | Title | Ref | Title |
|------|-------|------|-------|
| 6.3 | Backing off | 6.68 | When to coach |
| 6.8 | Checking for understanding | 6.12 | Coaching with others |
| 6.1 | Aiming high enough | 6.29 | Goal setting |
| 6.2 | Appraisals | 6.34 | Individual coaching |
| 6.6 | Building relationships | 6.37 | Learning and learning styles |
| 6.11 | Coaching outside work | 6.16 | Delegation |
| 6.61 | Teaching versus coaching | 6.48 | Planning to coach |
| 6.62 | Team coaching | 6.32 | 'I can't do it' |
| 6.64 | The past is a foreign country | 6.51 | Problems, problems, problems |
| 6.31 | Going the extra mile | 6.19 | Doing yourself out of a job |
| 6.4 | Being realistic | 6.25 | Following up |
| 6.9 | Checking your coachfulness | 6.5 | Being unrealistic |
| 6.13 | Coaching your boss | 6.15 | Coaching yourself |
| 6.14 | Coaching your peers | 6.35 | Killing fear |
| 6.17 | Developing the right environment | 6.40 | Letting go of the solution |
| 6.24 | Establishing the two-way process | 6.65 | The reluctant coach |
| 6.26 | From why to how | 6.54 | Quick results |
| 6.28 | Giving feedback | 6.55 | Reluctance to improve |
| 6.30 | Goals | 6.58 | Slow progress |
| 6.46 | 'Now look what you've done' | 6.59 | Stop and think |
| 6.47 | Overcoming a lifetime of learning | 6.44 | Mission |
| 6.66 | Using the ADAPT model | 6.60 | Strategy |
| 6.43 | Measuring improvement | 6.67 | Vision |
| 6.41 | Love | 6.20 | Eliminate the negative |
| 6.42 | Marking time | 6.23 | Establishing pace |
| 6.56 | Role models | 6.33 | 'If only they wouldn't…' |
| 6.22 | Engendering belief | 6.53 | Putting it into practice |
| 6.27 | Getting beneath anxiety | 6.63 | The future is a foreign country |
| 6.36 | Knowing what you know | 6.7 | Catch them doing it right |
| 6.38 | Learning to believe | 6.10 | Coaching as an organizational norm |
| 6.45 | Now is all you can do | | |
| 6.49 | Positive affirmations | 6.39 | Lecturing and hectoring |
| 6.50 | Positive visualization | 6.18 | Developing trust |
| 6.52 | Pushing and yielding | 6.21 | Emergencies |
| 6.57 | Sharing what you know | 6.69 | Wu wei |